The Clandestine Marriage by George Colman the Elder

A Comedy. As it is Acted at the Theatre-Royal in Drury-Lane

Written in collaboration with DAVID GARRICK

Huc adhibe vultus, et in unâ parce duobus:
Vivat, et ejusdem simus uterque parens!
Ovid

George Colman was born in Florence, Italy, in April 1732, where his father was stationed as British Resident Minister to the court of the Grand duke of Tuscany.

Before his first birthday Colman's father had died and his well-being was now in the hands of his Father's sister and her husband, William Pulteney, the later Lord Bath

Colman initially attended a private school in Marylebone before being sent to the exclusive Westminster School.

From there Colman went to Christ Church, Oxford. Whilst there he met Bonnell Thornton, the parodist, and together they founded 'The Connoisseur' periodical (1754–1756), which ran for 140 editions.

After taking his degree in 1755 Colman left Oxford and entered Lincoln's Inn. He was called to the bar in 1757. Despite a friendship forming with David Garrick and the promise of a literary career Colman decided that out of respect for Lord Bath he would continue to also practice law.

In 1760, Colman produced his first play, 'Polly Honeycomb'. It was a great success. The following year, 1761, he followed up with 'The Jealous Wife', a comedy partly founded on Henry Fielding's 'Tom Jones'. It made Colman famous.

On 21st October 1762 his son, George Colman the Younger, was born. He too would follow in his fathers' footsteps in education and career.

In 1764 with the death of Lord Bath and a substantial inheritance Colman was now financially secure and could also stop his law career to work solely on literature.

In 1765, his metrical translation of the six plays of Terence was published. The following year, 1766, in partnership with David Garrick, came another success: 'The Clandestine Marriage'. The only blot was when Colman quarreled with Garrick's refusal to take the part of Lord Ogleby.

With the arrival of 1767 Colman decided to expand his interests by acquiring a quarter share in the Covent Garden Theatre. When his play 'The Oxonian in Town' was performed there on 9th November that year a riot ensued, apparently sparked by a claque of card-sharpers.

Colman was elected to the Literary Club, in 1768, then nominally consisting of twelve members. In 1771 Thomas Arne's masque 'The Fairy Prince' premièred at Covent Garden, for which Colman wrote the libretto.

His instincts as a theatrical impresario were sound. As well as part-owner he was also the acting manager of Covent Garden for seven years during which he produced several 'adapted' plays of Shakespeare. He also directed the première of 'She Stoops to Conquer' in 1773.

In 1774 he sold to James Leake his share of Covent Garden, which had involved him in much litigation with his partners, and three years later, in 1777, he purchased the little theatre in the Haymarket from Samuel Foote.

George Colman suffered badly from attacks of paralysis in 1785 and his health became both failing and a burden. By 1789 his brain had become affected, and he died on 14th August 1794. He was buried in Kensington Church.

Index of Contents

Advertisement

Hogarth's Marriage-a-la-mode has before furnished Materials to the Author of a Novel, published some Years ago, under the Title of The Marriage-Act: But as that Writer persued a very different Story, and as his Work was chiefly designed for a Political Satire, very little Use could be made of it for the Service of this Comedy.

In Justice to the Person, who has been considered as the sole Author, the Party, who has hitherto lain concealed, thinks it incumbent on him to declare, that the Disclofure of his Name was, by his own Desire, reserved till the Publication of the Piece.

Both the Authors, however, who have before been separately honoured with the Indulgence of the Publick, now beg Leave to make their joint Acknowledgements for the very favourable Reception of the Clandestine Marriage.

Dramatis Personæ

Lord Ogleby	Mr. King.
Sir John Melvil	Mr. Holland.
Sterling	Mr. Yates.
Lovewell	Mr. Powell.
Canton	Mr. Baddeley.
Brush	Mr. Palmer.
Serjeant Flower	Mr. Love.
Traverse	Mr. Lee.
Trueman	Mr. Aickin.
Mrs. Heidelberg	Mrs. Clive.
Miss Sterling	Miss Pope.
Fanny	Mrs. Palmer.
Betty	Mrs. —
Chambermaid	Miss. Plym.
Trusty	Miss. Mills.

PROLOGUE

Written by Mr GARRICK

Spoken by Mr HOLLAND

Poets and Painters, who from Nature draw
Their best and richest Stores, have made this Law:
That each should neighbourly assist his Brother,
And steal with Decency from one another.
To-night, your matchless Hogarth gives the Thought,
Which from his Canvas to the Stage is brought.
And who so fit to warm the Poet's Mind,
As he who pictur'd Morals and Mankind?
But not the same their Characters and Scenes;
Both labour for one End, by different Means:
Each, as it suits him, takes a separate Road,
Their one great Object, Marriage-a-la-mode!
Where Titles deign with Cits to have and hold,

And change rich Blood for more substantial Gold!
And honour'd Trade from Interest turns aside,
To hazard Happiness for titled Pride.
The Painter dead, yet still he charms the Eye;
While England lives, his Fame can never die:
But he, who struts his Hour upon the Stage,
Can scarce extend his Fame for Half an Age;
Nor Pen nor Pencil can the Actor save,
The Art, and Artist, share one common Grave.
O let me drop one tributary Tear,
On poor Jack Falstaff's Grave, and Juliet's Bier!
You to their Worth must Testimony give;
'Tis in your Hearts alone their Fame can live.
Still as the Scenes of Life will shift away,
The strong Impressions of their Art decay.
Your Children cannot feel what you have known;
They'll boast of Quins and Cibbers of their own:
The greatest Glory of our happy few,
Is to be felt, and be approv'd by you.

ACT I

SCENE: A room in Sterling's house

MISS FANNY and **BETTY** meeting.

BETTY [Running in]
Ma'am! Miss Fanny! Ma'am!

FANNY
What's the matter! Betty!

BETTY
Oh la! Ma'am! as sure as I'm alive, here is your husband—

FANNY
Hush! my dear Betty! if any body in the house should hear you, I am ruined.

BETTY
Mercy on me! it has frighted me to such a degree, that my heart is come up to my mouth.—But as I was a saying, Ma'am, here's that dear, sweet—

FANNY
Have a care! Betty.

BETTY

Lord! I'm bewitched, I think.—But as I was a saying, Ma'am, here's Mr. Lovewell just come from London.

FANNY
Indeed!

BETTY
Yes, indeed, and indeed, Ma'am, he is. I saw him crossing the court-yard in his boots.

FANNY
I am glad to hear it.—But pray now, my dear Betty, be cautious. Don't mention that word again on any account. You know, we have agreed never to drop any expressions of that sort for fear of an accident.

BETTY
Dear Ma'am, you may depend upon me. There is not a more trustier creature on the face of the earth, than I am. Though I say it, I am as secret as the grave—and if it's never told, till I tell it, it may remain untold till doom's-day for Betty.

FANNY
I know you are faithful—but in our circumstances we cannot be too careful.

BETTY
Very true, Ma'am!—and yet I vow and protest, there's more plague than pleasure with a secret; especially if a body mayn't mention it to four or five of one's particular acquaintance.

FANNY
Do but keep this secret a little while longer, and then, I hope you may mention it to any body.—Mr. Lovewell will acquaint the family with the nature of our situation as soon as possible.

BETTY
The sooner, the better, I believe: for if he does not tell it, there's a little tell-tale, I know of, will come and tell it for him.

FANNY [Blushing]
Fie, Betty!

BETTY
Ah! you may well blush.—But you're not so sick, and so pale, and so wan, and so many qualms—

FANNY
Have done! I shall be quite angry with you.

BETTY
Angry!—Bless the dear puppet! I am sure I shall love it, as much as if it was my own.—I meant no harm, heaven knows.

FANNY
Well—say no more of this—It makes me uneasy—All I have to ask of you, is to be faithful and secret, and not to reveal this matter, till we disclose it to the family ourselves.

BETTY

Me reveal it!—if I say a word, I wish I may be burned. I wou'd not do you any harm for the world—And as for Mr. Lovewell, I am sure I have loved the dear gentleman ever since he got a tide-waiter's place for my brother—But let me tell you both, you must leave off your soft looks to each other, and your whispers, and your glances, and your always sitting next to one another at dinner, and your long walks together in the evening—For my part, if I had not been in the secret, I shou'd have known you were a pair of loviers at least, if not man and wife, as—

FANNY

See there now! again. Pray be careful.

BETTY

Well—well—nobody hears me.—Man and wife—I'll say so no more—what I tell you is very true for all that—

LOVEWELL [Calling within]
William!

BETTY

Hark! I hear your husband—

FANNY

What!

BETTY

I say, here comes Mr. Lovewell—Mind the caution I give you—I'll be whipped now, if you are not the first person he sees or speaks to in the family—However, if you chuse it, it's nothing at all to me—as you sow, you must reap—as you brew, so you must bake.—I'll e'en slip down the back-stairs, and leave you together.

[Exit.

FANNY [Alone]

I see, I see I shall never have a moment's ease till our marriage is made publick. New distresses croud in upon me every day. The sollicitude of my mind sinks my spirits, preys upon my health, and destroys every comfort of my life. It shall be revealed, let what will be the consequence.

[Enter **LOVEWELL**.

LOVEWELL

My love!—How's this?—In tears?—Indeed this is too much. You promised me to support your spirits, and to wait the determination of our fortune with patience.—For my sake, for your own, be comforted! Why will you study to add to our uneasiness and perplexity?

FANNY

Oh, Mr. Lovewell! The indelicacy of a secret marriage grows every day more and more shocking to me. I walk about the house like a guilty wretch: I imagine myself the object of the suspicion of the whole family; and am under the perpetual terrors of a shameful detection.

LOVEWELL

Indeed, indeed, you are to blame. The amiable delicacy of your temper, and your quick sensibility, only serve to make you unhappy.—To clear up this affair properly to Mr. Sterling, is the continual employment of my thoughts. Every thing now is in a fair train. It begins to grow ripe for a discovery; and I have no doubt of its concluding to the satisfaction of ourselves, of your father, and the whole family.

FANNY

End how it will, I am resolved it shall end soon—very soon.—I wou'd not live another week in this agony of mind to be mistress of the universe.

LOVEWELL

Do not be too violent neither. Do not let us disturb the joy of your sister's marriage with the tumult this matter may occasion!—I have brought letters from Lord Ogleby and Sir John Melvil to Mr. Sterling.—They will be here this evening—and, I dare say, within this hour.

FANNY

I am sorry for it.

LOVEWELL

Why so?

FANNY

No matter—Only let us disclose our marriage immediately!

LOVEWELL

As soon as possible.

FANNY

But directly.

LOVEWELL

In a few days, you may depend on it.

FANNY

To night—or to-morrow morning.

LOVEWELL

That, I fear, will be impracticable.

FANNY

Nay, but you must.

LOVEWELL

Must! why?

FANNY

Indeed, you must.—I have the most alarming reasons for it.

LOVEWELL

Alarming indeed! for they alarm me, even before I am acquainted with them—What are they?

FANNY

I cannot tell you.

LOVEWELL

Not tell me?

FANNY

Not at present. When all is settled, you shall be acquainted with every thing.

LOVEWELL

Sorry they are coming!—Must be discovered!—What can this mean!—Is it possible you can have any reasons that need be concealed from me?

FANNY

Do not disturb yourself with conjectures—but rest assured, that though you are unable to divine the cause, the consequence of a discovery, be it what it will, cannot be attended with half the miseries of the present interval.

LOVEWELL

You put me upon the rack.—I wou'd do any thing to make you easy.—But you know your father's temper.—Money (you will excuse my frankness) is the spring of all his actions, which nothing but the idea of acquiring nobility or magnificence can ever make him forego—and these he thinks his money will purchase.—You know too your aunt's, Mrs. Heidelberg's, notions of the splendor of high life, her contempt for every thing that does not relish of what she calls Quality, and that from the vast fortune in her hands, by her late husband, she absolutely governs Mr. Sterling and the whole family: now, if they should come to the knowledge of this affair too abruptly, they might, perhaps, be incensed beyond all hopes of reconciliation.

FANNY

But if they are made acquainted with it otherwise than by ourselves, it will be ten times worse: and a discovery grows every day more probable. The whole family have long suspected our affection. We are also in the power of a foolish maid-servant; and if we may even depend on her fidelity, we cannot answer for her discretion.—Discover it therefore immediately, lest some accident should bring it to light, and involve us in additional disgrace.

LOVEWELL

Well—well—I meant to discover it soon, but would not do it too precipitately.—I have more than once sounded Mr. Sterling about it, and will attempt him more seriously the next opportunity. But my principal hopes are these.—My relationship to Lord Ogleby, and his having placed me with your father, have been, you know, the first links in the chain of this connection between the two families; in consequence of which, I am at present in high favour with all parties: while they all remain thus well-affected to me, I propose to lay our case before the old Lord; and if I can prevail on him to mediate in this affair, I make no doubt but he will be able to appease your father; and, being a lord and a man of quality, I am sure he may bring Mrs. Heidelberg into good-humour at any time.—Let me beg you, therefore, to have but a little patience, as, you see, we are upon the very eve of a discovery, that must probably be to our advantage.

FANNY
Manage it your own way. I am persuaded.

LOVEWELL
But in the mean time make yourself easy.

FANNY
As easy as I can, I will.—We had better not remain together any longer at present.—Think of this business, and let me know how you proceed.

LOVEWELL
Depend on my care! But, pray, be chearful.

FANNY
I will.

[As she is going out, Enter **STERLING**.

STERLING
Hey-day! who have we got here?

FANNY [Confused]
Mr. Lovewell, Sir!

STERLING
And where are you going, hussey!

FANNY
To my sister's chamber, Sir!

[Exit.

STERLING
Ah, Lovewell! What! always getting my foolish girl yonder into a corner!—Well—well—let us but once see her elder sister fast-married to Sir John Melvil, we'll soon provide a good husband for Fanny, I warrant you.

LOVEWELL
Wou'd to heaven, Sir, you would provide her one of my recommendation!

STERLING
Yourself? eh, Lovewell!

LOVEWELL
With your pleasure, Sir!

STERLING
Mighty well!

LOVEWELL
And I flatter myself, that such a proposal would not be very disagreeable to Miss Fanny.

STERLING
Better and better!

LOVEWELL
And if I could but obtain your consent, Sir,—

STERLING
What! you marry Fanny!—no—no—that will never do, Lovewell!—You're a good boy, to be sure—I have a great value for you—but can't think of you for a son-in-law.—There's no Stuff in the case, no money, Lovewell!

LOVEWELL
My pretensions to fortune, indeed, are but moderate: but though not equal to splendor, sufficient to keep us above distress.—Add to which, that I hope by diligence to increase it—and have love, honour—

STERLING
But not the Stuff, Lovewell!—Add one little round o to the sum total of your fortune, and that will be the finest thing you can say to me.—You know I've a regard for you—would do any thing to serve you—any thing on the footing of friendship—but—

LOVEWELL
If you think me worthy of your friendship, Sir, be assured, that there is no instance in which I should rate your friendship so highly.

STERLING
Psha! psha! that's another thing, you know.—Where money or interest is concerned, friendship is quite out of the question.

LOVEWELL
But where the happiness of a daughter is at stake, you wou'd not scruple, sure, to sacrifice a little to her inclinations.

STERLING
Inclinations! why, you wou'd not persuade me that the girl is in love with you—eh, Lovewell!

LOVEWELL
I cannot absolutely answer for Miss Fanny, Sir; but am sure that the chief happiness or misery of my life depends entirely upon her.

STERLING

Why, indeed now if your kinsman, Lord Ogleby, would come down handsomely for you—but that's impossible—No, no—'twill never do—I must hear no more of this—Come, Lovewell, promise me that I shall hear no more of this.

LOVEWELL [Hesitating]

I am afraid, Sir, I shou'd not be able to keep my word with you, if I did promise you.

STERLING

Why you wou'd not offer to marry her without my consent? wou'd you, Lovewell!

LOVEWELL [Confused]

Marry her, Sir!

STERLING

Ay, marry her, Sir!—I know very well that a warm speech or two from such a dangerous young spark, as you are, will go much farther towards persuading a silly girl to do what she has more than a month's mind to do, than twenty grave lectures from fathers or mothers, or uncles or aunts, to prevent her.—But you wou'd not, sure, be such a base fellow, such a treacherous young rogue, as to seduce my daughter's affections, and destroy the peace of my family in that manner.—I must insist on it, that you give me your word not to marry her without my consent.

LOVEWELL

Sir—I—I—as to that—I—I—I beg, Sir—Pray, Sir, excuse me on this subject at present.

STERLING

Promise then, that you will carry this matter no further without my approbation.

LOVEWELL

You may depend on it, Sir, that it shall go no further.

STERLING

Well—well—that's enough—I'll take care of the rest, I warrant you.—Come, come, let's have done with this nonsense!—What's doing in town?—Any news upon 'Change?

LOVEWELL

Nothing material.

STERLING

Have you seen the currants, the soap, and Madeira, safe in the warehouses? Have you compared the goods with the invoice and bills of lading, and are they all right?

LOVEWELL

They are, Sir!

STERLING

And how are stocks?

LOVEWELL

Fell one and an half this morning.

STERLING

Well—well—some good news from America, and they'll be up again.—But how are Lord Ogleby and Sir John Melvil? When are we to expect them?

LOVEWELL

Very soon, Sir! I came on purpose to bring you their commands. Here are letters from both of them.

[Giving letters.

STERLING

Let me see—let me see—'Slife, how his Lordship's letter is perfumed!—It takes my breath away.—
[Opening it]
And French paper too! with a fine border of flowers and flourishes—and a slippery gloss on it that dazzles one's eyes.—My dear Mr. Sterling.—
[Reading]
—Mercy on me! His Lorship writes a worse hand than a boy at his exercise—But how's this?—Eh!—with you to-night—
[Reading]
—Lawyers to-morrow morning—To-night!—that's sudden indeed.—Where's my sister Heidelberg? she shou'd know of this immediately.—Here John! Harry! Thomas!
[Calling the **SERVANTS**]
Hark ye, Lovewell!

LOVEWELL

Sir!

STERLING

Mind now, how I'll entertain his Lordship and Sir John—We'll shew your fellows at the other end of the town how we live in the city—They shall eat gold—and drink gold—and lie in gold—Here cook! butler!
[Calling]
What signifies your birth and education, and titles? Money, money, that's the stuff that makes the great man in this country.

LOVEWELL

Very true, Sir!

STERLING

True, Sir?—Why then have done with your nonsense of love and matrimony. You're not rich enough to think of a wife yet. A man of business shou'd mind nothing but his business.—Where are these fellows? John! Thomas!
[Calling]
—Get an estate, and a wife will follow of course.—Ah! Lovewell! an English merchant is the most respectable character in the universe. 'Slife, man, a rich English merchant may make himself a match for the daughter of a Nabob.—Where are all my rascals? Here, William!

[Exit calling.

LOVEWELL [Alone]

So!—As I suspected.—Quite averse to the match, and likely to receive the news of it with great displeasure.—What's best to be done?—Let me see!—Suppose I get Sir John Melvil to interest himself in this affair. He may mention it to Lord Ogleby with a better grace than I can, and more probably prevail on him to interfere in it. I can open my mind also more freely to Sir John. He told me, when I left him in town, that he had something of consequence to communicate, and that I could be of use to him. I am glad of it: for the confidence he reposes in me, and the service I may do him, will ensure me his good offices.—Poor Fanny! It hurts me to see her so uneasy, and her making a mystery of the cause adds to my anxiety.—Something must be done upon her account, for at all events, her sollicitude shall be removed.

[Exit.

SCENE: Changes to another chamber

Enter **MISS STERLING**, and **MISS FANNY**.

MISS STERLING

Oh, my dear sister, say no more! This is downright hypocrisy.—You shall never convince me that you don't envy me beyond measure.—Well, after all it is extremely natural—It is impossible to be angry with you.

FANNY

Indeed, sister, you have no cause.

MISS STERLING

And you really pretend not to envy me?

FANNY

Not in the least.

MISS STERLING

And you don't in the least wish that you was just in my situation?

FANNY

No, indeed, I don't. Why should I?

MISS STERLING

Why should you?—What! on the brink of marriage, fortune, title—But I had forgot.—There's that dear sweet creature Mr. Lovewell in the case.—You would not break your faith with your true love now for the world, I warrant you.

FANNY

Mr. Lovewell!—always Mr. Lovewell!—Lord, what signifies Mr. Lovewell? Sister!

Miss STERLING
Pretty peevish soul!—Oh, my dear, grave, romantick sister!—a perfect philosopher in petticoats!—Love and a cottage!—Eh, Fanny!—Ah, give me indifference and a coach and six!

FANNY
And why not the coach and six without the indifference?—But, pray, when is this happy marriage of your's to be celebrated?—I long to give you joy.

MISS STERLING
In a day or two—I can't tell exactly.—Oh, my dear sister!—I must mortify her a little.
[Aside]
—I know you have a pretty taste. Pray, give me your opinion of my jewels.—How d'ye like the stile of this esclavage?

[Shewing jewels.

FANNY
Extremely handsome indeed, and well fancied.

MISS STERLING
What d'ye think of these bracelets? I shall have a miniature of my father, set round with diamonds, to one, and Sir John's to the other.—And this pair of ear-rings! set transparent!—here, the tops, you see, will take off to wear in a morning, or in an undress—how d'ye like them?

[Shews jewels.

FANNY
Very much, I assure you—Bless me; sister, you have a prodigious quantity of jewels—you'll be the very Queen of Diamonds.

MISS STERLING
Ha! ha! ha! very well, my dear!—I shall be as fine as a little queen indeed.—I have a bouquet to come home to-morrow—made up of diamonds, and rubies, and emeralds, and topazes, and amethysts—jewels of all colours, green, red, blue, yellow, intermixt—the prettiest thing you ever saw in your life!—The jeweller says I shall set out with as many diamonds as any body in town, except Lady Brilliant, and Polly What d'ye-call-it, Lord Squander's kept mistress.

FANNY
But what are your wedding-cloaths, sister?

MISS STERLING
Oh, white and silver to be sure, you know.—I bought them at Sir Joseph Lutestring's, and sat above an hour in the parlour behind the shop, consulting Lady Lutestring about gold and silver stuffs, on purpose to mortify her.

FANNY

Fie, sister! how could you be so abominably provoking?

MISS STERLING
Oh, I have no patience with the pride of your city-knights' ladies.—Did you never observe the airs of Lady Lutestring drest in the richest brocade out of her husband's shop, playing crown-whist at Haberdasher's-Hall?—While the civil smirking Sir Joseph, with a smug wig trimmed round his broad face as close as a new-cut yew-hedge, and his shoes so black that they shine again, stands all day in his shop, fastened to his counter like a bad shilling?

FANNY
Indeed, indeed, sister, this is too much—If you talk at this rate, you will be absolutely a bye-word in the city—You must never venture on the inside of Temple-Bar again.

MISS STERLING
Never do I desire it—never, my dear Fanny, I promise you.—Oh, how I long to be transported to the dear regions of Grosvenor-Square—far—far from the dull districts of Aldersgate, Cheap, Candlewick, and Farringdon Without and Within!—My heart goes pit-a-pat at the very idea of being introduced at court!—gilt chariot!—pyeballed horses!—laced liveries!—and then the whispers buzzing round the circle—"Who is that young Lady! Who is she?"—"Lady Melvil, Ma'am!"—Lady Melvil! my ears tingle at the sound.—And then at dinner, instead of my farther perpetually asking—"Any news upon 'Change?"—to cry—well, Sir John! any thing new from Arthur's?—or—to say to some other woman of quality, was your Ladyship at the Dutchess of Rubber's last night?—Did you call in at Lady Thunder's? In the immensity of croud I swear I did not see you—scarce a soul at the opera last Saturday—shall I see you at Carlisle-House next Thursday?—Oh, the dear Beau-Monde! I was born to move in the sphere of the great world.

FANNY
And so, in the midst of all this happiness, you have no compassion for me—no pity for us poor mortals in common life.

MISS STERLING [Affectedly]
You?—You're above pity.—You would not change conditions with me—you're over head and ears in love, you know.—Nay, for that matter, if Mr. Lovewell and you come together, as I doubt not you will, you will live very comfortably, I dare say.—He will mind his business—you'll employ yourself in the delightful care of your family—and once in a season perhaps you'll sit together in a front-box at a benefit play, as we used to do at our dancing-master's, you know—and perhaps I may meet you in the summer with some other citizens at Tunbridge.—For my part, I shall always entertain a proper regard for my relations.—You sha'n't want my countenance, I assure you.

FANNY
Oh, you're too kind, sister!

[Enter **MRS HEIDELBERG**.

MRS HEIDELBERG [At entering]
Here this evening!—I vow and pertest we shall scarce have time to provide for them—Oh, my dear! [To **MISS STERLING**]
I am glad to see you're not quite in dish-abille. Lord Ogleby and Sir John Melvil will be here to-night.

MISS STERLING
To-night, Ma'am?

MRS HEIDELBERG
Yes, my dear, to-night.—Do, put on a smarter cap, and change those ordinary ruffles!—Lord, I have such a deal to do, I shall scarce have time to slip on my Italian lutestring.—Where is this dawdle of a housekeeper?—

[Enter **MRS TRUSTY**.

Oh, here, Trusty! do you know that people of qualaty are expected here this evening?

TRUSTY
Yes, Ma'am.

MRS HEIDELBERG
Well—Do you be sure now that every thing is done in the most genteelest manner—and to the honour of the famaly.

TRUSTY
Yes, Ma'am.

MRS HEIDELBERG
Well—but mind what I say to you.

TRUSTY
Yes, Ma'am.

MRS HEIDELBERG
His Lordship is to lie in the chintz bedchamber—d'ye hear?—And Sir John in the blue damask room—His Lordship's valet-de-shamb in the opposite—

TRUSTY
But Mr. Lovewell is come down—and you know that's his room, Ma'am.

MRS HEIDELBERG
Well—well—Mr. Lovewell may make shift—or get a bed at the George—But hark ye, Trusty!

TRUSTY
Ma'am!

MRS HEIDELBERG
Get the great dining-room in order as soon as possible. Unpaper the curtains, take the civers off the couch and the chairs, and put the china figures on the mantle-piece immediately.

TRUSTY
Yes, Ma'am.

MRS HEIDELBERG
Be gone then! fly, this instant!—Where's my brother Sterling—

TRUSTY
Talking to the butler, Ma'am.

MRS HEIDELBERG
Very well.

[Exit **TRUSTY**.

Miss Fanny!—I pertest I did not see you before—Lord, child, what's the matter with you?

FANNY
With me? Nothing, Ma'am.

MRS HEIDELBERG
Bless me! Why your face is as pale, and black, and yellow—of fifty colours, I pertest.—And then you have drest yourself as loose and as big—I declare there is not such a thing to be seen now, as a young woman with a fine waist—You all make yourselves as round as Mrs. Deputy Barter. Go, child!—You know the qualaty will be here by and by—Go, and make yourself a little more fit to be seen.

[Exit **MISS FANNY**.

She is gone away in tears—absolutely crying, I vow and pertest.—This ridicalous Love! we must put a stop to it. It makes a perfect nataral of the girl.

MISS STERLING [Affectedly]
Poor soul! she can't help it.

MRS HEIDELBERG
Well, my dear! Now I shall have an opportunity of convincing you of the absurdity of what you was telling me concerning Sir John Melvil's behaviour to you.

MISS STERLING
Oh, it gives me no manner of uneasiness. But, indeed, Ma'am, I cannot be persuaded but that Sir John is an extremely cold lover. Such distant civility, grave looks, and lukewarm professions of esteem for me and the whole family! I have heard of flames and darts, but Sir John's is a passion of mere ice and snow.

MRS HEIDELBERG
Oh, fie, my dear! I am perfectly ashamed of you. That's so like the notions of your poor sister! What you complain of as coldness and indifference, is nothing but the extreme gentilaty of his address, an exact pictur of the manners of qualaty.

MISS STERLING
Oh, he is the very mirror of complaisance! full of formal bows and set speeches!—I declare, if there was any violent passion on my side, I should be quite jealous of him.

MRS HEIDELBERG
I say jealus indeed—Jealus of who, pray?

MISS STERLING
My sister Fanny.
She seems a much greater favourite than I am, and he pays her infinitely more attention, I assure you.

MRS HEIDELBERG
Lord! d'ye think a man of fashion, as he is, can't distinguish between the genteel and the wulgar part of the famaly?—Between you and your sister, for instance—or me and my brother?—Be advised by me, child! It is all politeness and good-breeding.—Nobody knows the qualaty better than I do.

MISS STERLING
In my mind the old lord, his uncle, has ten times more gallantry about him than **SIR JOHN**
He is full of attentions to the ladies, and smiles, and grins, and leers, and ogles, and fills every wrinkle in his old wizen face with comical expressions of tenderness. I think he wou'd make an admirable sweetheart.

[Enter **STERLING**.

STERLING [At entering]
No fish?—Why the pond was dragged but yesterday morning—There's carp and tench in the boat.—Pox on't, if that dog Lovewell had any thought, he wou'd have brought down a turbot, or some of the land-carriage mackarel.

MRS HEIDELBERG
Lord, brother, I am afraid his lordship and Sir John will not arrive while it's light.

STERLING
I warrant you.—But, pray, sister Heidelberg, let the turtle be drest to-morrow, and some venison—and let the gardener cut some pine-apples—and get out some ice.—I'll answer for wine, I warrant you—I'll give them such a glass of Champagne as they never drank in their lives—no, not at a Duke's table.

MRS HEIDELBERG
Pray now, brother, mind how you behave. I am always in a fright about you with people of qualaty. Take care that you don't fall asleep directly after supper, as you commonly do. Take a good deal of snuff; that will keep you awake.—And don't burst out with your horrible loud horse-laughs. It is monstrous wulgar.

STERLING
Never fear, sister!—Who have we here?

MRS HEIDELBERG
It is Mons. Cantoon, the Swish gentleman, that lives with his Lordship, I vow and pertest.

[Enter **CANTON**.

STERLING

Ah, Mounseer! your servant.—I am very glad to see you, Mounseer.

CANTON

Mosh oblige to Mons. Sterling.—Ma'am, I am yours—Matemoiselle, I am yours.

[Bowing round.

MRS HEIDELBERG

Your humble servant, Mr. Cantoon!

CANTON

I kiss your hands, Matam!

STERLING

Well, Mounseer!—and what news of your good family!—when are we to see his Lordship and Sir John?

CANTON

Mons. Sterling! Milor Ogelby and Sir Jean Melvile will be here in one quarter-hour.

STERLING

I am glad to hear it.

MRS HEIDELBERG

O, I am perdigious glad to hear it. Being so late I was afeard of some accident.—Will you please to have any thing, Mr. Cantoon, after your journey?

CANTON

No, I tank you, Ma'am.

MRS HEIDELBERG

Shall I go and shew you the apartments, Sir?

CANTON

You do me great honeur, Ma'am.

MRS HEIDELBERG [To **MISS STERLING**]

Come then!—come, my dear!

[Exeunt.

[Manet **STERLING**.

STERLING

Pox on't, it's almost dark—It will be too late to go round the garden this evening.—However, I will carry them to take a peep at my fine canal at least, I am determined.

[Exit.

SCENE: An anti-chamber to Lord Ogleby's bed-chamber

Table with chocolate, and small case for medicines.

Enter **BRUSH**, my Lord's valet-de-chambre, and Sterling's **CHAMBER MAID**.

BRUSH
YOU shall stay, my dear, I insist upon it.

CHAMBER MAID
Nay, pray, Sir, don't be so positive; I can't stay indeed.

BRUSH
You shall take one cup to our better acquaintance.

CHAMBER MAID
I seldom drinks chocolate; and if I did, one has no satisfaction, with such apprehensions about one—if my Lord should wake, or the Swish gentleman should see one, or Madam Heidelberg should know of it, I should be frighted to death—besides I have had my tea already this morning—I'm sure I hear my Lord.

BRUSH
No, no, Madam, don't flutter yourself—the moment my Lord wakes, he rings his bell, which I answer sooner or later, as it suits my convenience.

CHAMBER MAID
But should he come upon us without ringing—

BRUSH
I'll forgive him if he does—This key—
[Takes a phial out of the case]
—locks him up till I please to let him out.

CHAMBER MAID
Law, Sir! that's potecary's-stuff.

BRUSH
It is so—but without this he can no more get out of bed—than he can read without spectacles—
[Sips]
What with qualms, age, rheumatism, and a few surfeits in his youth, he must have a great deal of brushing, oyling, screwing, and winding up to let him a going for the day.

CHAMBER MAID [Sips]
That's prodigious indeed—

[Sips]
My Lord seems quite in a decay.

BRUSH
Yes, he's quite a spectacle,
[Sips]
a mere corpse, till he is reviv'd and refresh'd from our little magazine here—When the restorative pills, and cordial waters warm his stomach, and get into his head, vanity frisks in his heart, and then he sets up for the lover, the rake, and the fine gentleman.

CHAMBER MAID [Sips]
Poor gentleman! [Frighten'd]
—but should the Swish gentleman come upon us.

BRUSH
Why then the English gentleman would be very angry—No foreigner must break in upon my privacy.
[Sips]
But I can assure you Monsieur Canton is otherwise employ'd—He is oblig'd to skim the cream of half a score news-papers for my Lord's breakfast—ha, ha, ha. Pray, Madam, drink your cup peaceably—My Lord's chocolate is remarkably good, he won't touch a drop but what comes from Italy.

CHAMBER MAID [Sipping]
'Tis very fine indeed!—
[Sips]
—and charmingly perfum'd—it smells for all the world like our young ladies dressing-boxes.

BRUSH
You have an excellent taste, Madam, and I must beg of you to accept of a few cakes for your own drinking,—
[Takes 'em out of a drawer in the table]
—and in return, I desire nothing but to taste the perfume of your lips—
[Kisses her]
—A small return of favours, Madam, will make, I hope, this country and retirement agreeable to both.
[He bows, she curtsies]
Your young ladies are fine girls, faith:—
[Sips]
tho' upon my soul, I am quite of my old lord's mind about them; and were I inclin'd to matrimony, I should take the youngest.
[Sips]

CHAMBER MAID
Miss Fanny's the most affablest and the most best nater'd creter!

BRUSH
And the eldest a little haughty or so—

CHAMBER MAID

More haughtier and prouder than Saturn himself—but this I say quite confidential to you, for one would not hurt a young lady's marriage, you know.

[Sips.

BRUSH
By no means, but you can't hurt it with us—we don't consider tempers—we want money, Mrs. Nancy—give us enough of that, we'll abate you a great deal in other particulars—ha, ha, ha.

CHAMBER MAID
Bless me, here's somebody—
[Bell rings]
—O! 'tis my Lord—Well, your servant, Mr. Brush—I'll clean the cups in the next room.

BRUSH
Do so—but never mind the bell—I shan't go this half hour.—Will you drink tea with me in the afternoon?

CHAMBER MAID
Not for the world, Mr. Brush—I'll be here to set all things to rights—but I must not drink tea indeed—and so your servant.

[Exit **CHAMBER MAID** with tea-board.

[Bell rings again.

BRUSH
It is impossible to stupify one's self in the country for a week without some little flirting with the Abigails:—this is much the handsomest wench in the house, except the old citizen's youngest daughter, and I have not time enough to lay a plan for Her—
[Bell rings]
And now I'll go to my Lord, for I have nothing else to do.

[Going.

[Enter **CANTON** with news-papers in his hand.

CANTON
Monsieur Brush—Maistre Brush—My Lor stirra yet?

BRUSH
He has just rung his bell—I am going to him.

CANTON
Depechez vous donc.

[Exit **BRUSH**.

[Puts on spectacles]

I wish de Deviel had all dese papiers—I forget, as fast as I read—De Advertise put out of my head de Gazette, de Gazette de Chronique, and so dey all go l'un apres l'autre—I must get some nouvelle for my Lor, or he'll be enragée contre moi—Voyons!—

[Reads in the papers]

Here is noting but Anti-Sejanus & advertise—

[Enter **CHAMBER MAID** with chocolate things.

Vat you vant, child?—

CHAMBER MAID

Only the chocolate things, Sir.

CANTON

O ver well—dat is good girl—and ver prit too!

[Exit **CHAMBER MAID**.

[**LORD OGLEBY** within.

LORD OGLEBY

Canton, he, he—

[Coughs]

—Canton!

CANTON

I come my Lor—vat shall I do?—I have no news—He vill make great tintamarre!—

LORD OGLEBY [Within]

Canton, I say, Canton! Where are you?—

[Enter **LORD OGLEBY** leaning on **BRUSH**.

CANTON

Here my Lor, I ask pardon my Lor, I have not finish de papiers—

LORD OGLEBY

Dem your pardon, and your papers—I want you here. Canton.

CANTON

Den I run, dat is all—

Shuffles along—**LORD OGLEBY** leans upon **CANTON** too, and comes forward.

LORD OGLEBY

You Swiss are the most unaccountable mixture—you have the language and the impertinence of the French, with the laziness of Dutchmen.

CANTON
'Tis very true, my Lor—I can't help—

LORD OGLEBY [Cries out]
O Diavolo!

CANTON
You are not in pain, I hope, my Lor.

LORD OGLEBY
Indeed but I am, my Lor—That vulgar fellow Sterling, with his city politeness, would force me down his slope last night to see a clay-colour'd ditch, which he calls a canal; and what with the dew, and the east-wind, my hips and shoulders are absolutely screw'd to my body.

CANTON
A littel veritable eau d'arquibusade vil set all to right again—

[My **LORD** sits down, **BRUSH** gives chocolate.

LORD OGLEBY
Where are the palsy-drops, Brush?

BRUSH
Here, my Lord!

[Pouring out.

LORD OGLEBY
Quelle nouvelle avez vous, Canton?

CANTON
A great deal of papier, but no news at all.

LORD OGLEBY
What! nothing at all, you stupid fellow?

CANTON
Yes, my Lor, I have littel advertise here vil give you more plaisir den all de lyes about noting at all. La voila!

[Puts on his spectacles.

LORD OGLEBY
Come read it, Canton, with good emphasis, and good discretion.

CANTON
I vil, my Lor—

[**CANTON** reads]

Dere is no question, but dat de Cosmetique Royale vil utterlie take away all heats, pimps, frecks & oder eruptions of de skin, and likewise de wrinque of old age, &c. &c.—A great deal more, my Lor—be sure to ask for de Cosmetique Royale, signed by de Docteur own hand—Dere is more raison for dis caution dan good men vil tink—Eh bien, my Lor!

LORD OGLEBY

Eh bien, Canton!—Will you purchase any?

CANTON

For you, my Lor?

LORD OGLEBY

For me, you old puppy! for what?

CANTON

My Lor?

LORD OGLEBY

Do I want cosmeticks?

CANTON

My Lor!

LORD OGLEBY

Look in my face—come, be sincere—Does it want the assistance of art?

CANTON [With his spectacles]

En veritè, non.—'Tis very smoose and brillian—but I tote dat you might take a little by way of prevention.

LORD OGLEBY

You thought like an old fool, Monsieur, as you generally do—The surfeit-water, Brush!

[**BRUSH** pours out.

What do you think, Brush, of this family, we are going to be connected with?—Eh!

BRUSH

Very well to marry in, my Lord; but it would not do to live with.

LORD OGLEBY

You are right, Brush—There is no washing the Blackamoor white—Mr. Sterling will never get rid of Black-Fryars, always taste of the Borachio—and the poor woman his sister is so busy and so notable, to make one welcome, that I have not got over her first reception; it almost amounted to suffocation! I think the daughters are tolerable—Where's my cephalick snuff?

[**BRUSH** gives him a box.

CANTON
Dey tink so of you, my Lor, for dey look at noting else, ma foi.

LORD OGLEBY
Did they?—Why, I think they did a little—Where's my glass?

[**BRUSH** puts one on the table.

The youngest is delectable.

[Takes snuff.

CANTON
O, ouy, my Lor—very delect, inteed; she made doux yeux at you, my Lor.

LORD OGLEBY
She was particular—the eldest, my nephew's lady, will be a most valuable wife; she has all the vulgar spirits of her father, and aunt, happily blended with the termagant qualities of her deceased mother.— Some pepper-mint water, Brush!—How happy is it, Cant, for young ladies in general, that people of quality overlook every thing in a marriage contract but their fortune.

CANTON
C'est bien heureux, et commode aussi.

LORD OGLEBY
Brush, give me that pamphlet by my bed-side—

[**BRUSH** goes for it.

Canton, do you wait in the anti-chamber, and let nobody interrupt me till I call you.

CANTON
Mush goot may do your Lorship!

LORD OGLEBY [To **BRUSH**, who brings the pamphlet]
And now, Brush, leave me a little to my studies.

[Exit **BRUSH**.

LORD OGLEBY [Alone]
What can I possibly do among these women here, with this confounded rheumatism? It is a most grievous enemy to gallantry and address—
[Gets off his chair]
—He!—Courage, my Lor! by heav'ns, I'm another creature—
[Hums and dances a little]
It will do, faith—Bravo, my Lor! these girls have absolutely inspir'd me—If they are for a game of romps—Me voila pret!

[Sings and dances]

O—that's an ugly twinge—but it's gone—I have rather too much of the lily this morning in my complexion; a faint tincture of the rose will give a delicate spirit to my eyes for the day.

[Unlocks a drawer at the bottom of the glass, and takes out rouge; while he's painting himself, a knocking at the door.

Who's there! I won't be disturb'd.

CANTON [Without]
My Lor, my Lor, here is Monsieur Sterling to pay his devoir to you this morn in your chambre.

LORD OGLEBY [Softly]
What a fellow!—
[Aloud]
I am extreamly honour'd by Mr. Sterling—Why don't you see him in, Monsieur?—I wish he was at the bottom of his stinking canal—
[Door opens]
Oh, my dear Mr. Sterling, you do me a great deal of honour.

[Enter **STERLING** and **LOVEWELL**.

STERLING
I hope, my Lord, that your Lordship slept well in the night—I believe there are no better beds in Europe than I have—I spare no pains to get 'em, nor money to buy 'em—His Majesty, God bless him, don't sleep upon a better out of his palace; and if I had said in too, I hope no treason, my Lord.

LORD OGLEBY
Your beds are like every thing else about you, incomparable!—They not only make one rest well, but give one spirits, Mr. Sterling.

STERLING
What say you then, my Lord, to another walk in the garden? You must see my water by day-light, and my walks, and my slopes, and my clumps, and my bridge, and my flow'ring trees, and my bed of Dutch tulips—Matters look'd but dim last night, my Lord; I feel the dew in my great toe—but I would put on a cut shoe that I might be able to walk you about—I may be laid up to-morrow.

LORD OGLEBY [Aside]
I pray heav'n you may!

STERLING
What say you, my Lord!

LORD OGLEBY
I was saying, Sir, that I was in hopes of seeing the young ladies at breakfast: Mr. Sterling, they are, in my mind, the finest tulips in this part of the world—he, he.

CANTON

Bravissimo, my Lor!—ha, ha, he.

STERLING
They shall meet your Lordship in the garden—we won't lose our walk for them; I'll take you a little round before breakfast, and a larger before dinner, and in the evening you shall go the Grand Tower, as I call it, ha, ha, ha.

LORD OGLEBY
Not a foot, I hope, Mr. Sterling—consider your gout, my good friend—You'll certainly be laid by the heels for your politeness—he, he, he.

CANTON
Ha, ha, ha—'tis admirable! en veritè!—

[Laughing very heartily.

STERLING
If my young man—
[To **LOVEWELL**]
—here, would but laugh at my jokes, which he ought to do, as Mounseer does at yours, my Lord, we should be all life and mirth.

LORD OGLEBY
What say you, Cant, will you take my kinsman under your tuition? you have certainly the most companionable laugh I ever met with, and never out of tune.

CANTON
But when your lorship is out of spirits.

LORD OGLEBY
Well said, Cant,—but here comes my nephew, to play his part.

[Enter **SIR JOHN MELVIL**.

Well, Sir John, what news from the island of Love? have you been sighing and serenading this morning?

SIR JOHN
I am glad to see your Lordship in such spirits this morning.

LORD OGLEBY
I'm sorry to see you so dull, Sir—What poor things, Mr. Sterling, these very young fellows are! they make love with faces, as if they were burying the dead—though, indeed, a marriage sometimes may be properly called a burying of the living—eh, Mr. Sterling?—

STERLING
Not if they have enough to live upon, my Lord—Ha, ha, ha.

CANTON

Dat is all Monsieur Sterling tink of.

SIR JOHN
Prithee, Lovewell, come with me into the garden; I have something of consequence for you, and I must communicate it directly.

LOVEWELL
We'll go together—
If your Lordship and Mr. Sterling please, we'll prepare the ladies to attend you in the garden.

[Exeunt **SIR JOHN**, and **LOVEWELL**.

STERLING
My girls are always ready, I make 'em rise soon, and to-bed early; their husbands shall have 'em with good constitutions, and good fortunes, if they have nothing else, my Lord.

LORD OGLEBY
Fine things, Mr. Sterling!

STERLING
Fine things, indeed, my Lord!—Ah, my Lord, had not you run off your speed in your youth, you had not been so crippled in your age, my Lord.

LORD OGLEBY [Half-laughing]
Very pleasant, I protest, He, he, he.—

STERLING
Here's Mounseer now, I suppose, is pretty near your Lordship's standing; but having little to eat, and little to spend, in his own country, he'll wear three of your Lordship out—eating and drinking kills us all.

LORD OGLEBY [Aside]
Very pleasant, I protest—What a vulgar dog!

CANTON
My Lor so old as me!—He is shicken to me—and look like a boy to pauvre me.

STERLING
Ha, ha, ha. Well said, Mounseer—keep to that, and you'll live in any country of the world—Ha, ha, ha.— But, my Lord, I will wait upon you into the garden; we have but a little time to breakfast—I'll go for my hat and cane, fetch a little walk with you, my Lord, and then for the hot rolls and butter!

Exit **STERLING**.

LORD OGLEBY
I shall attend you with pleasure—Hot rolls and butter, in July!—I sweat with the thoughts of it—What a strange beast it is!

CANTON

C'est un barbare.

LORD OGLEBY
He is a vulgar dog, and if there was not so much money in the family, which I can't do without, I would leave him and his hot rolls and butter directly—Come along, Monsieur!

[Exeunt **LORD OGLEBY** and **CANTON**.

SCENE: Scene changes to the Garden

Enter **SIR JOHN MELVIL**, and **LOVEWELL**.

LOVEWELL
In my room this morning? Impossible.

SIR JOHN
Before five this morning, I promise you.

LOVEWELL
On what occasion?

SIR JOHN
I was so anxious to disclose my mind to you, that I could not sleep in my bed—But I found that you could not sleep neither—The bird was flown, and the nest long since cold.—Where was you, Lovewell?

LOVEWELL
Pooh! prithee! ridiculous!

SIR JOHN
Come now! which was it? Miss Sterling's maid? a pretty little rogue!—or Miss Fanny's Abigail? a sweet soul too!—or—

LOVEWELL
Nay, nay, leave trifling, and tell me your business.

SIR JOHN
Well, but where was you, Lovewell?

LOVEWELL
Walking—writing—what signifies where I was?

SIR JOHN
Walking! yes, I dare say. It rained as hard as it could pour. Sweet refreshing showers to walk in! No, no, Lovewell.—Now would I give twenty pounds to know which of the maids—

LOVEWELL

But your business! your business, Sir John!

SIR JOHN
Let me a little into the secrets of the family.

LOVEWELL
Psha!

SIR JOHN
Poor Lovewell! he can't bear it, I see. She charged you not to kiss and tell.—Eh, Lovewell! However, though you will not honour me with your confidence, I'll venture to trust you with mine.—What d'ye think of Miss Sterling?

LOVEWELL
What do I think of Miss Sterling?

SIR JOHN
Ay; what d'ye think of her?

LOVEWELL
An odd question!—but I think her a smart, lively girl, full of mirth and sprightliness.

SIR JOHN
All mischief and malice, I doubt.

LOVEWELL
How?

SIR JOHN
But her person—what d'ye think of that?

LOVEWELL
Pretty and agreeable.

SIR JOHN
A little grisette thing.

LOVEWELL
What is the meaning of all this?

SIR JOHN
I'll tell you. You must know, Lovewell, that notwithstanding all appearances—
[Seeing **LORD OGLEBY** &c.]
We are interrupted—When they are gone, I'll explain.

[Enter **LORD OGLEBY**, **STERLING**, **MRS HEIDELBERG**, **MISS STERLING**, and **FANNY**.

LORD OGLEBY

Great improvements indeed, Mr. Sterling! wonderful improvements! The four seasons in lead, the flying Mercury, and the basin with Neptune in the middle, are all in the very extreme of fine taste. You have as many rich figures as the man at Hyde-Park Corner.

STERLING
The chief pleasure of a country house is to make improvements, you know, my Lord. I spare no expence, not I.—This is quite another-guess sort of a place than it was when I first took it, my Lord. We were surrounded with trees. I cut down above fifty to make the lawn before the house, and let in the wind and the sun—smack-smooth—as you see.—Then I made a green-house out of the old laundry, and turned the brew-house into a pinery.—The high octagon summer-house, you see yonder, is raised on the mast of a ship, given me by an East-India captain, who has turned many a thousand of my money. It commands the whole road. All the coaches and chariots, and chaises, pass and repass under your eye. I'll mount you up there in the afternoon, my Lord. 'Tis the pleasantest place in the world to take a pipe and a bottle,—and so you shall say, my Lord.

LORD OGLEBY
Ay—or a bowl of punch, or a can of flip, Mr. Sterling! for it looks like a cabin in the air.—If flying chairs were in use, the captain might make a voyage to the Indies in it still, if he had but a fair wind.

CANTON
Ha! ha! ha! ha!

MRS HEIDELBERG
My brother's a little comacal in his ideas, my Lord!—But you'll excuse him.—I have a little gothic dairy, fitted up entirely in my own taste.—In the evening I shall hope for the honour of your Lordship's company to take a dish of tea there, or a sullabub warm from the cow.

LORD OGLEBY
I have every moment a fresh opportunity of admiring the elegance of Mrs. Heidelberg—the very flower of delicacy, and cream of politeness.

MRS HEIDELBERG
O my Lord!

LORD OGLEBY
O Madam!

STERLING
How d'ye like these close walks, my Lord?

LORD OGLEBY
A most excellent serpentine! It forms a perfect maze, and winds like a true-lover's knot.

STERLING
Ay—here's none of your strait lines here—but all taste—zig-zag—crinkum crankum—in and out—right and left—to and again—twisting and turning like a worm, my Lord!

LORD OGLEBY

Admirably laid out indeed, Mr. Sterling! one can hardly see an inch beyond one's nose any where in these walks.—You are a most excellent œconomist of your land, and make a little go a great way.—It lies together in as small parcels as if it was placed in pots out at your window in Gracechurch-Street.

CANTON
Ha! ha! ha! ha!

LORD OGLEBY
What d'ye laugh at, Canton?

CANTON
Ah! que cette similitude est drole! So clever what you say, mi Lor!

LORD OGLEBY [To **FANNY**]
You seem mightly engaged, Madam. What are those pretty hands so busily employed about?

FANNY
Only making up a nosegay, my Lord!—Will your Lordship do me the honour of accepting it?

[Presenting it.

LORD OGLEBY [Apart]
I'll wear it next my heart, Madam!—I see the young creature doats on me.

MISS STERLING
Lord, sister! you've loaded his Lordship with a bunch of flowers as big as the cook or the nurse carry to town on Monday morning for a beaupot.—Will your Lordship give me leave to present you with this rose and a sprig of sweet-briar?

LORD OGLEBY
The truest emblems of yourself, Madam! all sweetness and poignancy.—A little jealous, poor soul!

[Apart.

STERLING
Now, my Lord, if you please, I'll carry you to see my Ruins.

MRS HEIDELBERG
You'll absolutely fatigue his Lordship with overwalking, Brother!

LORD OGLEBY
Not at all, Madam! We're in the garden of Eden, you know; in the region of perpetual spring, youth, and beauty.

[Leering at the **WOMEN**.

MRS HEIDELBERG [Apart]
Quite the man of qualaty, I pertest.

CANTON
Take a my arm, mi Lor!

[**LORD OGLEBY** leans on him.

STERLING
I'll only shew his Lordship my ruins, and the cascade, and the Chinese bridge, and then we'll go in to breakfast.

LORD OGLEBY
Ruins, did you say, Mr. Sterling?

STERLING
Ay, ruins, my Lord! and they are reckoned very fine ones too. You would think them ready to tumble on your head. It has just cost me a hundred and fifty pounds to put my ruins in thorough repair.—This way, if your Lordship pleases.

LORD OGLEBY [Going, stops]
What steeple's that we see yonder? the parish-church, I suppose.

STERLING
Ha! ha! ha! that's admirable. It is no church at all, my Lord! it is a spire that I have built against a tree, a field or two off, to terminate the prospect. One must always have a church, or an obelisk, or a something, to terminate the prospect, you know. That's a rule in taste, my Lord!

LORD OGLEBY
Very ingenious, indeed! For my part, I desire no finer prospect, than this I see before me.
[Leering at the **WOMEN**]
—Simple, yet varied; bounded, yet extensive.—Get away, Canton!
[Pushing away **CANTON**]
I want no assistance.—I'll walk with the ladies.

STERLING
This way, my Lord!

LORD OGLEBY
Lead on, Sir!—We young folks here will follow you.—Madam!—Miss Sterling!—Miss Fanny! I attend you.

[Exit, after **STERLING**, gallanting the **LADIES**.

CANTON [Following]
He is cock o'de game, ma foy!

[Exit.

[Manent **SIR JOHN MELVIL**, and **LOVEWELL**.

SIR JOHN

At length, thank heaven, I have an opportunity to unbosom.—I know you are faithful, Lovewell, and flatter myself you would rejoice to serve me.

LOVEWELL

Be assured, you may depend on me.

SIR JOHN

You must know then, notwithstanding all appearances, that this treaty of marriage between Miss Sterling and me will come to nothing.

LOVEWELL

How!

SIR JOHN

It will be no match, Lovewell.

LOVEWELL

No match?

SIR JOHN

No.

LOVEWELL

You amaze me. What should prevent it?

SIR JOHN

I.

LOVEWELL

You! wherefore?

SIR JOHN

I don't like her.

LOVEWELL

Very plain indeed! I never supposed that you was extremely devoted to her from inclination, but thought you always considered it as a matter of convenience, rather than affection.

SIR JOHN

Very true. I came into the family without any impressions on my mind—with an unimpassioned indifference ready to receive one woman as soon as another. I looked upon love, serious, sober love, as a chimæra, and marriage as a thing of course, as you know most people do. But I, who was lately so great an infidel in love, am now one of its sincerest votaries.—In short, my defection from Miss Sterling proceeds from the violence of my attachment to another.

LOVEWELL

Another! So! so! here will be fine work. And pray who is she?

SIR JOHN
Who is she! who can she be? but Fanny, the tender, amiable, engaging Fanny.

LOVEWELL
Fanny! What Fanny?

SIR JOHN
Fanny Sterling. Her sister—Is not she an angel, Lovewell?

LOVEWELL
Her sister? Confusion!—You must not think of it, Sir John.

SIR JOHN
Not think of it? I can think of nothing else. Nay, tell me, Lovewell! was it possible for me to be indulged in a perpetual intercourse with two such objects as Fanny and her sister, and not find my heart led by insensible attraction towards Her?—You seem confounded—Why don't you answer me?

LOVEWELL
Indeed, Sir John, this event gives me infinite concern.

SIR JOHN
Why so?—Is not she an angel, Lovewell?

LOVEWELL
I foresee that it must produce the worst consequences. Consider the confusion it must unavoidably create. Let me persuade you to drop these thoughts in time.

SIR JOHN
Never—never, Lovewell!

LOVEWELL
You have gone too far to recede. A negotiation, so nearly concluded, cannot be broken off with any grace. The lawyers, you know, are hourly expected; the preliminaries almost finally settled between Lord Ogleby and Mr. Sterling; and Miss Sterling herself ready to receive you as a husband.

SIR JOHN
Why the banns have been published, and nobody has forbidden them, 'tis true—but you know either of the parties may change their minds even after they enter the church.

LOVEWELL
You think too lightly of this matter. To carry your addresses so far—and then to desert her—and for her sister too!—It will be such an affront to the family, that they can never put up with it.

SIR JOHN
I don't think so: for as to my transferring my passion from her to her sister, so much the better!—for then, you know, I don't carry my affections out of the family.

LOVEWELL
Nay, but prithee be serious, and think better of it.

SIR JOHN
I have thought better of it already, you see. Tell me honestly, Lovewell! can you blame me? Is there any comparison between them?

LOVEWELL
As to that now—why that—that is just—just as it may strike different people. There are many admirers of Miss Sterling's vivacity.

SIR JOHN
Vivacity! a medley of Cheapside pertness, and Whitechapel pride.—No—no—if I do go so far into the city for a wedding-dinner, it shall be upon turtle at least.

LOVEWELL
But I see no probability of success; for granting that Mr. Sterling wou'd have consented to it at first, he cannot listen to it now. Why did not you break this affair to the family before?

SIR JOHN
Under such embarrassed circumstances as I have been, can you wonder at my irresolution or perplexity? Nothing but despair, the fear of losing my dear Fanny, cou'd bring me to a declaration even now; and yet, I think I know Mr. Sterling so well, that, strange as my proposal may appear, if I can make it advantageous to him as a money-transaction, as I am sure I can, he will certainly come into it.

LOVEWELL
But even suppose he should, which I very much doubt, I don't think Fanny herself wou'd listen to your addresses.

SIR JOHN
You are deceived a little in that particular.

LOVEWELL
You'll find I am in the right.

SIR JOHN
I have some little reason to think otherwise.

LOVEWELL
You have not declared your passion to her already?

SIR JOHN
Yes, I have.

LOVEWELL
Indeed!—And—and—and how did she receive it?

SIR JOHN

I think it is not very easy for me to make my addresses to any woman, without receiving some little encouragement.

LOVEWELL

Encouragement! did she give you any encouragement?

SIR JOHN

I don't know what you call encouragement—but she blushed—and cried—and desired me not to think of it any more:—upon which I prest her hand—kissed it—swore she was an angel—and I cou'd see it tickled her to the soul.

LOVEWELL

And did she express no surprise at your declaration?

SIR JOHN

Why, faith, to say the truth, she was a little surprised—and she got away from me too, before I cou'd thoroughly explain myself. If I should not meet with an opportunity of speaking to her, I must get you to deliver a letter from me.

LOVEWELL

I!—a letter!—I had rather have nothing—

SIR JOHN

Nay, you promised me your assistance—and I am sure you cannot scruple to make yourself useful on such an occasion.—You may, without suspicion, acquaint her verbally of my determined affection for her, and that I am resolved to ask her father's consent.

LOVEWELL

As to that, I—your commands, you know—that is, if she—Indeed, Sir John, I think you are in the wrong.

SIR JOHN

Well—well—that's my concern—Ha! there she goes, by heaven! along that walk yonder, d'ye see?—I'll go to her immediately.

LOVEWELL

You are too precipitate. Consider what you are doing.

SIR JOHN

I wou'd not lose this opportunity for the universe.

LOVEWELL [Detaining him]

Nay, pray don't go! Your violence and eagerness may overcome her spirits.—The shock will be too much for her.

SIR JOHN

Nothing shall prevent me.—Ha! now she turns into another walk.—Let me go!
[Breaks from him]

I shall lose her.—

[Going, turns back]

Be sure now to keep out of the way—If you interrupt us, I shall never forgive you.

[Exit hastily.

LOVEWELL [Alone]

'Sdeath! I can't bear this. In love with my wife! acquaint me with his passion for her! make his addresses before my face!—I shall break out before my time.—This was the meaning of Fanny's uneasiness. She could not encourage him—I am sure she could not.—Ha! they are turning into the walk, and coming this way.—Shall I leave the place?—Leave him to sollicit my wife! I can't submit to it.—They come nearer and nearer—If I stay it will look suspicious—It may betray us, and incense him—They are here—I must go—I am the most unfortunate fellow in the world.

[Exit.

[Enter **FANNY**, and **SIR JOHN**.

FANNY

Leave me, Sir John, I beseech you leave me!—nay, why will you persist to follow me with idle sollicitations, which are an affront to my character, and an injury to your own honour?

SIR JOHN

I know your delicacy, and tremble to offend it: but let the urgency of the occasion be my excuse! Consider Madam, that the future happiness of my life depends on my present application to you! consider that this day must determine my fate; and these are perhaps the only moments left me to incline you to warrant my passion, and to intreat you not to oppose the proposals I mean to open to your father.

FANNY

For shame, for shame, Sir John! Think of your previous engagements! Think of your own situation, and think of mine!—What have you discovered in my conduct that might encourage you to so bold a declaration? I am shocked that you should venture to say so much, and blush that I should even dare to give it a hearing.—Let me be gone!

SIR JOHN

Nay, stay Madam! but one moment!—Your sensibility is too great.—Engagements! what engagements have even been pretended on either side than those of family-convenience? I went on in the trammels of matrimonial negotiation with a blind submission to your father and Lord Ogleby; but my heart soon claimed a right to be consulted. It has devoted itself to you, and obliges me to plead earnestly for the same tender interest in your's.

FANNY

Have a care, Sir John! do not mistake a depraved will for a virtuous inclination. By these common pretences of the heart, half of our sex are made fools, and a greater part of yours despise them for it.

SIR JOHN

Affection, you will allow, is involuntary. We cannot always direct it to the object on which it should fix—But when it is once inviolably attached, inviolably as mine is to you, it often creates reciprocal affection.—When I last urged you on this subject, you heard me with more temper, and I hoped with some compassion.

FANNY
You deceived yourself. If I forbore to exert a proper spirit, nay if I did not even express the quickest resentment of your behaviour, it was only in consideration of that respect I wish to pay you, in honour to my sister: and be assured Sir, woman as I am, that my vanity could reap no pleasure from a triumph, that must result from the blackest treachery to her.

[Going.

SIR JOHN
One word, and I have done.
[Stopping her]
—Your impatience and anxiety, and the urgency of the occasion, oblige me to be brief and explicit with you.—I appeal therefore from your delicacy to your justice.—Your sister, I verily believe, neither entertains any real affection for me, or tenderness for you.—Your father, I am inclined to think, is not much concerned by means of which of his daughters the families are united.—Now as they cannot, shall not be connected, otherwise than by my union with you, why will you, from a false delicacy, oppose a measure so conducive to my happiness, and, I hope, your own?—I love you, most passionately and sincerely love you—and hope to propose terms agreeable to Mr. Sterling.—If then you don't absolutely loath, abhor, and scorn me if there is no other happier man—

FANNY
Hear me, Sir! hear my final determination.—Were my father and sister as insensible as you are pleased to represent them;—were my heart for ever to remain disengaged to any other—I could not listen to your proposals.—What! You on the very eve of a marriage with my sister; I living under the same roof with her, bound not only by the laws of friendship and hospitality, but even the ties of blood, to contribute to her happiness,—and not to conspire against her peace—the peace of a whole family—and that my own too!—Away! away, Sir John!—At such a time, and in such circumstances, your addresses only inspire me with horror.—Nay, you must detain me no longer.—I will go.

SIR JOHN
Do not leave me in absolute despair!—Give me a glimpse of hope!

[Falling on his knees.

FANNY
I cannot. Pray, Sir John!

[Struggling to go.

SIR JOHN
Shall this hand be given to another?
[Kissing her hand]
No—I cannot endure it.—My whole soul is yours, and the whole happiness of my life is in your power.

[Enter **MISS STERLING**.

FANNY
Ha! my sister is here. Rise for shame, Sir John!

SIR JOHN [Rising]
Miss Sterling!

MISS STERLING
I beg pardon, Sir!—You'll excuse me, Madam!—I have broke in upon you a little unopportunely, I believe—But I did not mean to interrupt you—I only came, Sir, to let you know that breakfast waits, if you have finished your morning's devotions.

SIR JOHN
I am very sensible, Miss Sterling, that this may appear particular, but—

MISS STERLING
Oh dear, Sir John, don't put yourself to the trouble of an apology. The thing explains itself.

SIR JOHN
It will soon, Madam!—In the mean time I can only assure you of my profound respect and esteem for you, and make no doubt of convincing Mr. Sterling of the honour and integrity of my intentions. And—and—your humble servant, Madam!

[Exit in confusion.

[Manent **FANNY**, and **MISS STERLING**.

MISS STERLING
Respect?—Insolence!—Esteem?—Very fine truly!—And you, Madam! my sweet, delicate, innocent, sentimental sister! will you convince my papa too of the integrity of your intentions?

FANNY
Do not upbraid me, my dear sister! Indeed, I don't deserve it. Believe me, you can't be more offended at his behaviour than I am, and I am sure it cannot make you half so miserable.

MISS STERLING
Make me miserable! You are mightily deceived, Madam! It gives me no sort of uneasiness, I assure you.—A base fellow!—As for you, Miss! the pretended softness of your disposition, your artful good-nature, never imposed upon me. I always knew you to be sly, and envious, and deceitful.

FANNY
Indeed you wrong me.

MISS STERLING

Oh, you are all goodness, to be sure!—Did not I find him on his knees before you? Did not I see him kiss your sweet hand? Did not I hear his protestations? Was not I witness of your dissembled modesty?—No—no, my dear! don't imagine that you can make a fool of your elder sister so easily.

FANNY
Sir John, I own, is to blame; but I am above the thoughts of doing you the least injury.

MISS STERLING
We shall try that, Madam!—I hope, Miss, you'll be able to give a better account to my papa and my aunt—for they shall both know of this matter, I promise you.

[Exit.

FANNY [Alone]
How unhappy I am! my distresses multiply upon me.—Mr. Lovewell must now become acquainted with Sir John's behaviour to me—and in a manner that may add to his uneasiness.—My father, instead of being disposed by fortunate circumstances to forgive any transgression, will be previously incensed against me.—My sister and my aunt will become irreconcilably my enemies, and rejoice in my disgrace.—Yet, at all events, I am determined on a discovery. I dread it, and am resolved to hasten it. It is surrounded with more horrors every instant, as it appears every instant more necessary.

[Exit.

ACT III

SCENE I

A hall

Enter a **SERVANT** leading in **SERJEANT FLOWER**, and Counsellors **TRAVERSE** and **TRUEMAN**—all booted.

SERVANT
This way, if you please, gentlemen! my master is at breakfast with the family at present—but I'll let him know, and he will wait on you immediately.

FLOWER
Mighty well, young man, mighty well.

SERVANT
Please to favour me with your names, gentlemen.

FLOWER
Let Mr. Sterling know, that Mr. Serjeant Flower, and three other gentlemen of the bar, are come to wait on him according to his appointment.

SERVANT [Going]

I will, Sir.

FLOWER
And harkee, young man!

[**SERVANT** returns.

Desire my servant—Mr. Serjeant Flower's servant—to bring in my green and gold saddle-cloth and pistols, and lay them down here in the hall with my portmanteau.

SERVANT
I will, Sir.

[Exit.

[Manent **LAWYERS**.

FLOWER
Well, gentlemen! the settling these marriage articles falls conveniently enough, almost just on the eve of the circuits.—Let me see—the Home, the Midland, Oxford, and Western,—ay, we can all cross the country well enough to our several destinations.—Traverse, when do you begin at Abingdon?

TRAVERSE
The day after to-morrow.

FLOWER
That is commission-day with us at Warwick too.—But my clerk has retainers for every cause in the paper, so it will be time enough if I am there the next morning.—Besides, I have about half a dozen cases that have lain by me ever since the spring assizes, and I must tack opinions to them before I see my country-clients again—so I will take the evening before me—and then currente calamo, as I say—eh, Traverse!

TRAVERSE
True, Mr. Serjeant.

FLOWER
Do You expect to have much to do on the Home circuit these assizes?

TRAVERSE
Not much nisi prius business, but a good deal on the crown side, I believe.—The goals are brimfull—and some of the felons in good circumstances, and likely to be tolerable clients.—Let me see! I am engag'd for three highway robberies, two murders, one forgery, and half a dozen larcenies, at Kingston.

FLOWER
A pretty decent goal-delivery!—Do you expect to bring off Darkin, for the robbery on Putney-Common? Can you make out your alibi?

TRAVERSE

Oh, no! the crown witnesses are sure to prove our identity. We shall certainly be hanged: but that don't signify.—But, Mr. Serjeant, have you much to do?—any remarkable cause on the Midland this circuit?

FLOWER
Nothing very remarkable,—except two rapes, and Rider and Western at Nottingham, for crim. con.—but, on the whole, I believe a good deal of business.—Our associate tells me, there are above thirty venires for Warwick.

TRAVERSE
Pray, Mr. Serjeant, are you concerned in Jones and Thomas at Lincoln?

FLOWER
I am—for the plaintiff.

TRAVERSE
And what do you think on't?

FLOWER
A nonsuit.

TRAVERSE
I thought so.

FLOWER
Oh, no manner of doubt on't—luce clarius—we have no right in us—we have but one chance.

TRAVERSE
What's that?

FLOWER
Why, my Lord Chief does not go the circuit this time, and my brother Puzzle being in the commission, the cause will come on before him.

TRUEMAN
Ay, that may do, indeed, if you can but throw dust in the eyes of the defendant's council.

FLOWER [To **TRUEMAN**]
True.—Mr. Trueman, I think you are concerned for Lord Ogleby in this affair?

TRUEMAN
I am, Sir—I have the honour to be related to his Lordship, and hold some courts for him in Somersetshire,—go the Western circuit—and attend the sessions at Exeter, merely because his Lordship's interest and property lie in that part of the kingdom.

FLOWER
Ha!—and pray, Mr. Trueman, how long have you been called to the bar?

TRUEMAN

About nine years and three quarters.

FLOWER
Ha!—I don't know that I ever had the pleasure of seeing you before.—I wish you success, young gentleman!

[Enter **STERLING**.

STERLING
Oh, Mr. Serjeant Flower, I am glad to see you—Your servant, Mr. Serjeant! gentlemen, your servant!— Well, are all matters concluded? Has that snail-paced conveyancer, old Ferret of Gray's Inn, settled the articles at last? Do you approve of what he has done? Will his tackle hold? tight and strong?—Eh, master Serjeant?

FLOWER
My friend Ferret's slow and sure, Sir—But then, serius aut citius, as we say,—sooner or later, Mr. Sterling, he is sure to put his business out of hand as he should do.—My clerk has brought the writings, and all other instruments along with him, and the settlement is, I believe, as good a settlement as any settlement on the face of the earth!

STERLING
But that damn'd mortgage of 60,000 l.—There don't appear to be any other incumbrances, I hope?

TRAVERSE
I can answer for that, Sir—and that will be cleared off immediately on the payment of the first part of Miss Sterling's portion—You agree, on your part, to come down with 80,000 l.—

STERLING
Down on the nail.—Ay, ay, my money is ready to-morrow if he pleases—he shall have it in India-bonds, or notes, or how he chuses.—Your lords, and your dukes, and your people at the court-end of the town stick at payments sometimes—debts unpaid, no credit lost with them—but no fear of us substantial fellows—eh, Mr. Serjeant!—

FLOWER
Sir John having last term, according to agreement, levied a fine, and suffered a recovery, has thereby cut off the entail of the Ogleby estate for the better effecting the purposes of the present intended marriage; on which above-mentioned Ogleby estate, a jointure of 2000 l. per ann. is secured to your eldest daughter, now Elizabeth Sterling, spinster, and the whole estate, after the death of the aforesaid earl, descends to the heirs male of Sir John Melvil on the body of the aforefaid Elizabeth Sterling lawfully to be begotten.

TRAVERSE
Very true—and Sir John is to be put in immediate possession of as much of his Lordship's Somersetshire estate, as lies in the manors of Hogmore and Cranford, amounting to between two and three thousands per ann. and at the death of Mr. Sterling, a further sum of seventy thousand—

[Enter **SIR JOHN MELVIL**.

STERLING

Ah, Sir John! Here we are—hard at it—paving the road to matrimony—We'll have no jolts; all upon the nail, as easy as the new pavement.—First the lawyers, then comes the doctor—Let us but dispatch the long-robe, we shall soon set Pudding-sleeves to work, I warrant you.

SIR JOHN

I am sorry to interrupt you, Sir—but I hope that both you and these gentlemen will excuse me—having something very particular for your private ear, I took the liberty of following you, and beg you will oblige me with an audience immediately.

STERLING

Ay, with all my heart—Gentlemen, Mr. Serjeant, you'll excuse it—Business must be done, you know.— The writings will keep cold till to-morrow morning.

FLOWER

I must be at Warwick, Mr. Sterling, the day after.

STERLING

Nay, nay, I shan't part with you to-night, gentlemen, I promise you—My house is very full, but I have beds for you all, beds for your servants, and stabling for all your horses.—Will you take a turn in the garden, and view some of my improvements before dinner? Or will you amuse yourselves in the green, with a game of bowls and a cool tankard?—My servants shall attend you—Do you chuse any other refreshment?—Call for what you please;—do as you please;—make yourselves quite at home, I beg of you.—Here,—Thomas, Harry, William, wait on these Gentlemen!—
[Follows the **LAWYERS** out, bawling and talking, and then returns to **SIR JOHN**]
And now, Sir, I am entirely at your service.—What are your commands with me, Sir John?

SIR JOHN

After having carried the negotiation between our families to so great a length, after having assented so readily to all your proposals, as well as received so many instances of your chearful compliance with the demands made on our part, I am extremely concerned, Mr. Sterling, to be the involuntary cause of any uneasiness.

STERLING

Uneasiness! what uneasiness?—Where business is transacted as it ought to be, and the parties understand one another, there can be no uneasiness. You agree, on such and such conditions to receive my daughter for a wife; on the same conditions I agree to receive you as a son-in-law; and as to all the rest, it follows of course, you know, as regularly as the payment of a bill after acceptance.

SIR JOHN

Pardon me, Sir; more uneasiness has arisen than you are aware of. I am myself, at this instant, in a state of inexpressible embarrassment; Miss Sterling, I know, is extremely disconcerted too; and unless you will oblige me with the assistance of your friendship, I foresee the speedy progress of discontent and animosity through the whole family.

STERLING

What the deuce is all this? I don't understand a single syllable.

SIR JOHN

In one word then—it will be absolutely impossible for me to fulfill my engagements in regard to Miss Sterling.

STERLING

How, Sir John? Do you mean to put an affront upon my family? What! refuse to—

SIR JOHN

Be assured, Sir, that I neither mean to affront, nor forsake your family.—My only fear is, that you should desert me; for the whole happiness of my life depends on my being connected with your family by the nearest and tenderest ties in the world.

STERLING

Why, did not you tell me, but a moment ago, that it was absolutely impossible for you to marry my daughter?

SIR JOHN

True.—But you have another daughter, Sir—

STERLING

Well?

SIR JOHN

Who has obtained the most absolute dominion over my heart. I have already declared my passion to her; nay, Miss Sterling herself is also apprized of it, and if you will but give a sanction to my present addresses, the uncommon merit of Miss Sterling will no doubt recommend her to a person of equal, if not superior rank to myself, and our families may still be allied by my union with Miss Fanny.

STERLING

Mighty fine, truly! Why, what the plague do you make of us, Sir John? Do you come to market for my daughters, like servants at a statute-fair? Do you think that I will suffer you, or any man in the world, to come into my house, like the Grand Signior, and throw the handkerchief first to one, and then to t'other, just as he pleases? Do you think I drive a kind of African slave-trade with them? and—

SIR JOHN

A moment's patience, Sir! Nothing but the excess of my passion for Miss Fanny shou'd have induced me to take any step that had the least appearance of disrespect to any part of your family; and even now I am desirous to atone for my transgression, by making the most adequate compensation that lies in my power.

STERLING

Compensation! what compensation can you possibly make in such a case as this, Sir John?

SIR JOHN

Come, come, Mr. Sterling; I know you to be a man of sense, a man of business, a man of the world. I'll deal frankly with you; and you shall see that I do not desire a change of measures for my own gratification, without endeavouring to make it advantageous to you.

STERLING

What advantage can your inconstancy be to me, Sir John?

SIR JOHN

I'll tell you, Sir.—You know that by the articles at present subsisting between us, on the day of my marriage with Miss Sterling, you agree to pay down the gross sum of eighty thousand pounds.

STERLING

Well!

SIR JOHN

Now if you will but consent to my waving that marriage—

STERLING

I agree to your waving that marriage? Impossible, Sir John!

SIR JOHN

I hope not, Sir; as on my part, I will agree to wave my right to thirty thousand pounds of the fortune I was to receive with her.

STERLING

Thirty thousand, d'ye say?

SIR JOHN

Yes, Sir; and accept of Miss Fanny with fifty thousand, instead of fourscore.

STERLING

Fifty thousand—[Pausing]

SIR JOHN

Instead of fourscore.

STERLING

Why,—why,—there may be something in that.—Let me see; Fanny with fifty thousand instead of Betsey with fourscore—But how can this be, Sir John?—For you know I am to pay this money into the hands of my Lord Ogleby; who, I believe—between you and me, Sir John,—is not overstocked with ready money at present; and threescore thousand of it, you know, is to go to pay off the present incumbrances on the estate, Sir John.

SIR JOHN

That objection is easily obviated.—Ten of the twenty thousand, which would remain as a surplus of the fourscore, after paying off the mortgage, was intended by his Lordship for my use, that we might set off with some little eclat on our marriage; and the other ten for his own.—Ten thousand pounds therefore I shall be able to pay you immediately; and for the remaining twenty thousand you shall have a mortgage on that part of the estate which is to be made over to me, with whatever security you shall require for the regular payment of the interest, 'till the principal is duly discharged.

STERLING

Why—to do you justice, Sir John, there is something fair and open in your proposal; and since I find you do not mean to put an affront upon the family—

SIR JOHN

Nothing was ever farther from my thoughts, Mr. Sterling.—And after all, the whole affair is nothing extraordinary—such things happen every day—and as the world has only heard generally of a treaty between the families, when this marriage takes place, nobody will be the wiser, if we have but discretion enough to keep our own counsel.

STERLING

True, true; and since you only transfer from one girl to the other, it is no more than transferring so much stock, you know.

SIR JOHN

The very thing.

STERLING

Odso! I had quite forgot. We are reckoning without our host here. There is another difficulty—

SIR JOHN

You alarm me. What can that be?

STERLING

I can't stir a step in this business without consulting my sister Heidelberg.—The family has very great expectations from her, and we must not give her any offence.

SIR JOHN

But if you come into this measure, surely she will be so kind as to consent—

STERLING

I don't know that—Betsey is her darling, and I can't tell how far she may resent any slight that seems to be offered to her favourite neice.—However, I'll do the best I can for you.—You shall go and break the matter to her first, and by that time that I may suppose that your rhetorick has prevailed on her to listen to reason, I will step in to reinforce your arguments.

SIR JOHN

I'll fly to her immediately: you promise me your assistance?

STERLING

I do.

SIR JOHN [Going]

Ten thousand thanks for it! and now success attend me!

STERLING

Harkee, Sir John!

[**SIR JOHN** returns.

STERLING
Not a word of the thirty thousand to my sister, Sir John.

SIR JOHN [Going]
Oh, I am dumb, I am dumb, Sir.

STERLING
You remember it is thirty thousand.

SIR JOHN [Going]
To be sure I do.

STERLING
But Sir John!—one thing more.
[**SIR JOHN** returns]
My Lord must know nothing of this stroke of friendship between us.

SIR JOHN
Not for the world.—Let me alone! let me alone!

[Offering to go.

STERLING [Holding him]
—And when every thing is agreed, we must give each other a bond to be held fast to the bargain.

SIR JOHN
To be sure. A bond by all means! a bond, or whatever you please.

[Exit hastily.

STERLING [Alone]
I should have thought of more conditions—he's in a humour to give me every thing—Why, what mere children are your fellows of quality; that cry for a plaything one minute, and throw it by the next! as changeable as the weather, and as uncertain as the flocks.—Special fellows to drive a bargain! and yet they are to take care of the interest of the nation truly!—Here does this whirligig man of fashion offer to give up thirty thousand pounds in hard money, with as much indifference as if it was a china orange.—By this mortgage, I shall have a hold on his Terra-firma, and if he wants more money, as he certainly will,—let him have children by my daughter or no, I shall have his whole estate in a net for the benefit of my family.—Well; thus it is, that the children of citizens, who have acquired fortunes, prove persons of fashion; and thus it is, that persons of fashion, who have ruined their fortunes, reduce the next generation to cits.

[Exit.

SCENE: Changes to another apartment

[Enter **MRS HEIDELBERG**, and **MISS STERLNG**.

MISS STERLING
This is your gentle-looking, soft-speaking, sweet-smiling, affable Miss Fanny for you!

MRS HEIDELBERG
My Miss Fanny! I disclaim her. With all her arts she never could insinuat herself into my good graces—and yet she has a way with her, that deceives man, woman, and child, except you, and me, neice.

MISS STERLING
O ay; she wants nothing but a crook in her hand, and a lamb under her arm, to be a perfect picture of innocence and simplicity.

MRS HEIDELBERG
Just as I was drawn at Amsterdam, when I went over to visit my husband's relations.

MISS STERLING
And then she's so mighty good to servants pray, John, do this—pray, Tom, do that—thank you, Jenny—and then so humble to her relations—to be sure, Papa!—as my Aunt pleases—my Sister knows best—But with all her demurness and humility she has no objection to be Lady Melvil, it seems, nor to any wickedness that can make her so.

MRS HEIDELBERG
She Lady Melville? Compose yourself, Niece! I'll ladyship her indeed:—a little creepin, cantin—She shan't be the better for a farden of my money. But tell me, child, how does this intriguing with Sir John correspond with her partiality to Lovewell? I don't see a concatunation here.

MISS STERLING
There I was deceived, Madam. I took all their whisperings and stealing into corners to be the mere attraction of vulgar minds; but, behold! their private meetings were not to contrive their own insipid happiness, but to conspire against mine.—But I know whence proceeds Mr. Lovewell's resentment to me. I could not stoop to be familiar with my father's clerk, and so I have lost his interest.

MRS HEIDELBERG
My spurrit to a T.—My dear child!
[Kissing her]
—Mr. Heidelberg lost his election for member of parliament, because I would not demean myself to be slobbered about by drunken shoemakers, beastly cheesemongers, and greasy butchers and tallow-chandlers. However, Niece, I can't help diffuring a little in opinon from you in this matter. My experunce and sagucity makes me still suspect, that there is something more between her and that Lovewell, notwithstanding this affair of Sir John—I had my eye upon them the whole time of breakfast.—Sir John, I observed, looked a little confounded, indeed, though I knew nothing of what had passed in the garden. You seemed to sit upon thorns too: but Fanny and Mr. Lovewell made quite another-guess sort of a figur; and were as perfet a pictur of two distrest lovers, as if it had been drawn by Raphael Angelo.—As to Sir John and Fanny, I want a matter of fact.

MISS STERLING

Matter of fact, Madam! Did not I come unexpectedly upon them? Was not Sir John kneeling at her feet, and kissing her hand? Did not he look all love, and she all confusion? Is not that matter of fact? And did not Sir John, the moment that Papa was called out of the room to the lawyer-men, get up from breakfast, and follow him immediately? And I warrant you that by this time he has made proposals to him to marry my sister—Oh, that some other person, an earl, or a duke, would make his addresses to me, that I might be revenged on this monster!

MRS HEIDELBERG
Be cool, child! you shall be Lady Melvil, in spite of all their caballins, if it costs me ten thousand pounds to turn the scale. Sir John may apply to my brother, indeed; but I'll make them all know who governs in this fammaly.

MISS STERLING
As I live, Madam, yonder comes Sir John. A base man! I can't endure the sight of him. I'll leave the room this instant.

MRS HEIDELBERG
Poor thing! Well, retire to your own chamber, child; I'll give it him, I warrant you; and by and by I'll come, and let you know all that has past between us.

MISS STERLING
Pray do, Madam! —
[Looking back]
—A vile wretch!

[Exit in a rage.

[Enter **SIR JOHN MELVIL**.

SIR JOHN
Your most obedient humble servant, Madam!

[Bowing very respectfully.

MRS HEIDELBERG
Your servant, Sir John!

[Dropping a half-curtsy, and pouting.

SIR JOHN
Miss Sterling's manner of quitting the room on my approach, and the visible coolness of your behaviour to me, Madam, convince me that she has acquainted you with what past this morning.

MRS HEIDELBERG [Pouting]
I am very sorry, Sir John, to be made acquainted with any thing that should induce me to change the opinon, which I could always wish to entertain of a person of quallaty.

SIR JOHN

It has always been my ambition to merit the best opinion from Mrs. Heidelberg; and when she comes to weigh all circumstances, I flatter myself—

MRS HEIDELBERG

You do flatter yourself, if you imagine that I can approve of your behaviour to my niece, Sir John.—And give me leave to tell you, Sir John, that you have been drawn into an action much beneath you, Sir John; and that I look upon every injury offered to Miss Betty Sterling, as an affront to myself, Sir John.

SIR JOHN

I would not offend you for the world, Madam! but when I am influenced by a partiality for another, however ill-founded, I hope your discernment and good sense will think it rather a point of honour to renounce engagements, which I could not fulfil so strictly as I ought; and that you will excuse the change in my inclinations, since the new object, as well as the first, has the honour of being your niece, Madam.

MRS HEIDELBERG

I disclaim her as a niece, Sir John; Miss Sterling disclaims her as a sister, and the whole fammaly must disclaim her, for her monstrus baseness and treachery.

SIR JOHN

Indeed she has been guilty of none, Madam. Her hand and heart are, I am sure, entirely at the disposal of yourself, and Mr. Sterling.

[Enter **STERLING** behind.

And if you should not oppose my inclinations, I am sure of Mr. Sterling's consent, Madam.

MRS HEIDELBERG

Indeed!

SIR JOHN

Quite certain, Madam.

STERLING [Behind]

So! they seem to be coming to terms already. I may venture to make my appearance.

MRS HEIDELBERG

To marry Fanny?

STERLING advances by degrees.

SIR JOHN

Yes, Madam.

MRS HEIDELBERG

My brother has given his consent, you say?

SIR JOHN

In the most ample manner, with no other restriction than the failure of your concurrence, Madam.—
[Sees **STERLING**]
—Oh, here's Mr. Sterling, who will confirm what I have told you.

MRS HEIDELBERG
What! have you consented to give up your own daughter in this manner, brother?

STERLING [Apart to **SIR JOHN**]
Give her up! no, not give her up, sister; only in case that you—Zounds, I am afraid you have said too much, Sir John.

MRS HEIDELBERG
Yes, yes. I see now that it is true enough what my niece told me. You are all plottin and caballin against her.—Pray, does Lord Ogleby know of this affair?

SIR JOHN
I have not yet made him acquainted with it, Madam.

MRS HEIDELBERG
No, I warrant you. I thought so.—And so his Lordship and myself truly, are not to be consulted 'till the last.

STERLING
What! did not you consult my Lord? Oh fie for shame, Sir John!

SIR JOHN
Nay, but Mr. Sterling—

MRS HEIDELBERG
We, who are the persons of most consequence and experunce in the two fammalies, are to know nothing of the matter, 'till the whole is as good as concluded upon. But his Lordship, I am sure, will have more generosaty than to countenance such a perceeding—And I could not have expected such behaviour from a person of your quallaty, Sir John.—And as for you, brother—

STERLING
Nay, nay, but hear me, sister!

MRS HEIDELBERG
I am perfetly ashamed of you—Have you no spurrit? no more concern for the honour of our fammaly than to consent—

STERLING
Consent?—I consent!—As I hope for mercy, I never gave my consent. Did I consent, Sir John?

SIR JOHN
Not absolutely, without Mrs. Heidelberg's concurrence. But in case of her approbation—

STERLING [To **MRS HEIDELBERG**]

Ay, I grant you, if my sister approved.—But that's quite another thing, you know.—

MRS HEIDELBERG
Your sister approve, indeed!—I thought you knew her better, brother Sterling!—What! approve of having your eldest daughter returned upon your hands, and exchanged for the younger?—I am surprized how you could listen to such a scandalus proposal.

STERLING
I tell you, I never did listen to it.—Did not I say that I would be governed entirely by my sister, Sir John?—And unless she agreed to your marrying Fanny—

MRS HEIDELBERG
I agree to his marrying Fanny? abominable! The man is absolutely out of his senses.—Can't that wise head of yours foresee the consequence of all this, brother Sterling? Will Sir John take Fanny without a fortune? No.—After you have settled the largest part of your property on your youngest daughter, can there be an equal portion left for the eldest? No.—Does not this overturn the whole systum of the fammaly? Yes, yes, yes. You know I was always for my niece Betsey's marrying a person of the very first quallaty. That was my maxum. And, therefore, much the largest settlement was of course to be made upon her.—As for Fanny, if she could, with a fortune of twenty or thirty thousand pounds, get a knight, or a member of parliament, or a rich common-council-man for a husband, I thought it might do very well.

SIR JOHN
But if a better match should offer itself, why should not it be accepted, Madam?

MRS HEIDELBERG
What! at the expence of her elder sister! Oh fie, Sir John!—How could you bear to hear of such an indignaty, brother Sterling?

STERLING
I! nay, I shan't hear of it, I promise you.—I can't hear of it indeed, Sir John.

MRS HEIDELBERG
But you have heard of it, brother Sterling. You know you have; and sent Sir John to propose it to me. But if you can give up your daughter, I shan't forsake my niece, I assure you. Ah! if my poor dear Mr. Heidelberg, and our sweet babes had been alive, he would not have behaved so.

STERLING [Apart to **SIR JOHN**]
Did I, Sir John? nay speak!—Bring me off, or we are ruined.

SIR JOHN
Why, to be sure, to speak the truth—

MRS HEIDELBERG
To speak the truth, I'm ashamed of you both. But have a care what you are about, brother! have a care, I say. The lawyers are in the house, I hear; and if every thing is not settled to my liking, I'll have nothing more to say to you, if I live these hundred years.—I'll go over to Holland, and settle with Mr.

Vanderspracken, my poor husband's first cousin; and my own fammaly shall never be the better for a farden of my money, I promise you.

[Exit.

[Manent **SIR JOHN**, and **STERLING**.

STERLING
I thought so, I knew she never would agree to it.

SIR JOHN
'Sdeath, how unfortunate! What can we do, Mr. Sterling?

STERLING
Nothing.

SIR JOHN
What! must our agreement break off, the moment it is made then?

STERLING
It can't be helped, Sir John. The family, as I told you before, have great expectations from my sister; and if this matter proceeds, you hear yourself that she threatens to leave us.—My brother Heidelberg was a warm man; a very warm man; and died worth a Plumb at least; a Plumb! ay, I warrant you, he died worth a Plumb and a half.

SIR JOHN
Well; but if I—

STERLING
And then, my sister has three or four very good mortgages, a deal of money in the three per cents. and old South-Sea annuities, besides large concerns in the Dutch and French funds.—The greatest part of all this she means to leave to our family.

SIR JOHN
I can only say, Sir—

STERLING
Why, your offer of the difference of thirty thousand, was very fair and handsome to be sure, Sir John.

SIR JOHN
Nay, but I am even willing to—

STERLING
Ay, but if I was to accept it against her will, I might lose above a hundred thousand; so, you see, the ballance is against you, Sir John.

SIR JOHN
But is there no way, do you think, of prevailing on Mrs. Heidelberg to grant her consent?

STERLING

I am afraid not.—However, when her passion is a little abated—for she's very passionate—you may try what can be done: but you must not use my name any more, Sir John.

SIR JOHN

Suppose I was to prevail on Lord Ogleby to apply to her, do you think that would have any influence over her?

STERLING

I think he would be more likely to persuade her to it, than any other person in the family. She has a great respect for Lord Ogleby. She loves a lord.

SIR JOHN

I'll apply to him this very day.—And if he should prevail on Mrs. Heidelberg, I may depend on your friendship, Mr. Sterling?

STERLING

Ay, ay, I shall be glad to oblige you, when it is in my power; but as the account stands now, you see it is not upon the figures. And so your servant, Sir John.

[Exit.

SIR JOHN [Alone]

What a situation am I in!—Breaking off with her whom I was bound by treaty to marry; rejected by the object of my affections; and embroiled with this turbulent woman, who governs the whole family.—And yet opposition, instead of smothering, increases my inclination. I must have her. I'll apply immediately to Lord Ogleby; and if he can but bring over the aunt to our party, her influence will overcome the scruples and delicacy of my dear Fanny, and I shall be the happiest of mankind.

[Exit.

ACT IV

SCENE I

A room

Enter **STERLING**, **MRS HEIDELBERG**, and **MISS STERLING**.

STERLING

What! will you send Fanny to town, sister?

MRS HEIDELBERG

To-morrow morning. I've given orders about it already.

STERLING
Indeed?

MRS HEIDELBERG
Positively.

STERLING
But consider, sister, at such a time as this, what an odd appearance it will have.

MRS HEIDELBERG
Not half so odd, as her behaviour, brother.—This time was intended for happiness, and I'll keep no incendaries here to destroy it. I insist on her going off to-morrow morning.

STERLING
I'm afraid this is all your doing, Betsey.

MISS STERLING
No indeed, Papa. My aunt knows that it is not.—For all Fanny's baseness to me, I am sure I would not do, or say any thing to hurt her with you or my aunt for the world.

MRS HEIDELBERG
Hold your tongue, Betsey!—I will have my way.—When she is packed off, every thing will go on as it should do. Since they are at their intrigues, I'll let them see that we can act with vigur on our part; and the sending her out of the way shall be the purlimunary step to all the rest of my perceedings.

STERLING
Well, but sister—

MRS HEIDELBERG
It does not signify talking, brother Sterling, for I'm resolved to be rid of her, and I will.—Come along, child!
[To **MISS STERLING**]
—The post-shay shall be at the door by six o'clock in the morning; and if Miss Fanny does not get into it, why I will, and so there's an end of the matter.

[Bounces out with **MISS STERLING**.

MRS HEIDELBERG
One word more, brother Sterling!—I expect that you will take your eldest daughter in your hand, and make a formal complaint to Lord Ogleby of Sir John Melvil's behaviour.—Do this, brother; shew a proper regard for the honour of your fammaly yourself, and I shall throw in my mite to the raising of it. If not— but now you know my mind. So act as you please, and take the consequences.

[Exit.

STERLING [Alone]
The devil's in the woman for tyranny—mothers, wives, mistresses, or sisters, they always will govern us.—As to my sister Heidelberg, she knows the strength of her purse, and domineers upon the credit of

it.—"I will do this"—and "you shall do that"—and "you must do t'other, or else the fammaly shan't have a farden of"—

[Mimicking]

—So absolute with her money!—but to say the truth, nothing but money can make us absolute, and so we must e'en make the best of her.

SCENE: Changes to the garden

Enter **LORD OGLEBY** and **CANTON**.

LORD OGLEBY
What! Mademoiselle Fanny to be sent away!—Why?—Wherefore?—What's the meaning of all this?

CANTON
Je ne scais pas.—I know noting of it.

LORD OGLEBY
It can't be; it shan't be. I protest against the measure. She's a fine girl, and I had much rather that the rest of the family were annihilated than that she should leave us.—Her vulgar father, that's the very abstract of 'Change-Alley—the aunt, that's always endeavouring to be a fine lady—and the pert sister, for ever shewing that she is one, are horrid company indeed, and without her would be intolerable. Ah, la petite Fanchon! she's the thing. Is n't she, Cant?

CANTON
Dere is very good sympatie entre vous, and dat young lady, mi Lor.

LORD OGLEBY
I'll not be left among these Goths and Vandals, your Sterlings, your Heidelbergs, and Devilbergs—If she goes, I'll positively go too.

CANTON
In de same post-chay, mi Lor? You have no object to dat I believe, nor Mademoiselle neider too—ha, ha, ha.

LORD OGLEBY
Prithee hold thy foolish tongue, Canton. Does thy Swiss stupidity imagine that I can see and talk with a fine girl without desires?—My eyes are involuntarily attracted by beautiful objects—I fly as naturally to a fine girl—

CANTON
As de fine girl to you, my Lor, ha, ha, ha; you alway fly togedre like un pair de pigeons.—

LORD OGLEBY
Like un pair de pigeons—

[Mocks him]

—Vous etes un sot, Mons. Canton—Thou art always dreaming of my intrigues, and never seest me badiner, but you suspect mischief, you old fool, you.

CANTON
I am fool, I confess, but not always fool in dat, my Lor, he, he, he.

LORD OGLEBY
He, he, he.—Thou art incorrigible, but thy absurdities amuse one—Thou art like my rappee here,— [Takes out his box]
—a most ridiculous superfluity, but a pinch of thee now and then is a most delicious treat.

CANTON
You do me great honeur, my Lor.

LORD OGLEBY
'Tis fact, upon my soul.—Thou art properly my cephalick snuff, and art no bad medicine against megrims, vertigoes, and profound thinking—ha, ha, ha.

CANTON
Your flatterie, my Lor, vil make me too prode.

LORD OGLEBY
The girl has some little partiality for me, to be sure: but prithee, Cant, is not that Miss Fanny yonder?

CANTON [Looking with a glass]
En veritè, 'tis she, my Lor—'tis one of de pigeons,—de pigeons d'amour.

LORD OGLEBY [Smiling]
Don't be ridiculous, you old monkey.

CANTON
I am monkeè, I am ole, but I have eye, I have ear, and a little understand, now and den.—

LORD OGLEBY
Taisez vous bête!

CANTON
Elle vous attend, my Lor.—She vil make a love to you.

LORD OGLEBY
Will she? Have at her then! A fine girl can't oblige me more.—Egad, I find myself a little enjouée—come along, Cant! she is but in the next walk—but there is such a deal of this damned crinkum-crankum, as Sterling calls it, that one sees people for half an hour before one can get to them—Allons, Mons. Canton, allons donc!

[Exeunt singing in French.

SCENE: Another part of the garden

LOVEWELL, and **FANNY**.

LOVEWELL
My dear Fanny, I cannot bear your distress; it overcomes all my resolutions, and I am prepared for the discovery.

FANNY
But how can it be effected before my departure?

LOVEWELL
I'll tell you.—Lord Ogleby seems to entertain a visible partiality for you; and notwithstanding the peculiarities of his behaviour, I am sure that he is humane at the bottom. He is vain to an excess; but withall extremely good-natured, and would do any thing to recommend himself to a lady.—Do you open the whole affair of our marriage to him immediately. It will come with more irresistible persuasion from you than from myself; and I doubt not but you'll gain his friendship and protection at once.—His influence and authority will put an end to Sir John's sollicitations, remove your aunt's and sister's unkindness and suspicions, and, I hope, reconcile your father and the whole family to our marriage.

FANNY
Heaven grant it! Where is my Lord?

LOVEWELL
I have heard him and Canton since dinner singing French songs under the great walnut-tree by the parlour door. If you meet with him in the garden, you may disclose the whole immediately.

FANNY
Dreadful as the task is, I'll do it.—Any thing is better than this continual anxiety.

LOVEWELL
By that time the discovery is made, I will appear to second you.—Ha! here comes my Lord.—Now, my dear Fanny, summon up all your spirits, plead our cause powerfully, and be sure of success.—

[Going.

FANNY
Ah, don't leave me!

LOVEWELL
Nay, you must let me.

FANNY
Well; since it must be so, I'll obey you, if I have the power. Oh Lovewell!

LOVEWELL

Consider, our situation is very critical. To-morrow morning is fixt for your departure, and if we lose this opportunity, we may wish in vain for another.—He approaches—I must retire.—Speak, my dear Fanny, speak, and make us happy!

[Exit.

FANNY [Alone]
Good heaven, what a situation am I in! what shall I do? what shall I say to him? I am all confusion.

[Enter **LORD OGLEBY**, and **CANTON**.

LORD OGLEBY
To see so much beauty so solitary, Madam, is a satire upon mankind, and 'tis fortunate that one man has broke in upon your reverie for the credit of our sex.—I say one, Madam, for poor Canton here, from age and infirmities, stands for nothing.

CANTON
Noting at all, inteed.

FANNY
Your Lordship does me great honour. I had a favour to request, my Lord!

LORD OGLEBY
A favour, Madam!—To be honoured with your commands, is an inexpressible favour done to me, Madam.

FANNY
If your Lordship could indulge me with the honour of a moment's—
[Aside]
—What is the matter with me?

LORD OGLEBY [To **CANTON**]
The girl's confus'd—he!—here's something in the wind faith—I'll have a tete-a-tete with her—allez vous en!

CANTON
I go—ah, pauvre Mademoiselle! my Lor, have pitié upon de poor pigeone!

LORD OGLEBY [Smiling]
I'll knock you down Cant, if you're impertinent.

CANTON
Den I mus avay—
[Shuffles along]
—You are mosh please, for all dat.

[Exit.

FANNY [Aside]

I shall sink with apprehension.

LORD OGLEBY

What a sweet girl!—she's a civiliz'd being, and atones for the barbarism of the rest of the family.

FANNY

My Lord! I—[She curtseys, and blushes.

LORD OGLEBY [Addressing her]

I look upon it, Madam, to be one of the luckiest circumstances of my life, that I have this moment the honour of receiving your commands, and the satisfaction of confirming with my tongue, what my eyes perhaps have but too weakly expressed—that I am literally—the humblest of your servants.

FANNY

I think myself greatly honoured, by your Lordship's partiality to me; but it distresses me, that I am obliged in my present situation to apply to it for protection.

LORD OGLEBY

I am happy in your distress, Madam, because it gives me an opportunity to shew my zeal. Beauty to me, is a religion, in which I was born and bred a bigot, and would die a martyr.—I'm in tolerable spirits, faith!

FANNY

There is not perhaps at this moment a more distressed creature than myself. Affection, duty, hope, despair, and a thousand different sentiments, are struggling in my bosom; and even the presence of your Lordship, to whom I have flown for protection, adds to my preplexity.

LORD OGLEBY

Does it, Madam?—Venus forbid!—My old fault; the devil's in me, I think, for perplexing young women. [Aside and smiling]
Take courage, Madam! dear Miss Fanny, explain.—You have a powerful advocate in my breast, I assure you—my heart, Madam—I am attached to you by all the laws of sympathy, and delicacy.—By my honour, I am.

FANNY

Then I will venture to unburthen my mind.—Sir John Melvil, my Lord, by the most misplaced, and mistimed declaration of affection for me, has made me the unhappiest of women.

LORD OGLEBY

How, Madam! Has Sir John made his addresses to you?

FANNY

He has, my Lord, in the strongest terms. But I hope it is needless to say, that my duty to my father, love to my sister, and regard to the whole family, as well as the great respect I entertain for your Lordship,—
[Curtseying]
—made me shudder at his addresses.

LORD OGLEBY

Charming girl!—Proceed, my dear Miss Fanny, proceed!

FANNY
In a moment—give me leave, my Lord!—But if what I have to disclose should be received with anger or displeafure—

LORD OGLEBY
Impossible, by all the tender powers!—Speak, I beseech you, or I shall divine the cause before you utter it.

FANNY
Then, my Lord, Sir John's addresses are not only shocking to me in themselves, but are more particularly disagreeable to me at this time, as—as—

[Hesitating.

LORD OGLEBY
As what, Madam?

FANNY
As—pardon my confusion—I am intirely devoted to another.

LORD OGLEBY
If this is not plain, the devil's in it—
[Aside]
But tell me, my dear Miss Fanny, for I must know, tell me the how, the when, and the where—Tell me—

[Enter **CANTON** hastily.

CANTON
My Lor, my Lor, my Lor!—

LORD OGLEBY
Damn your Swiss impertinence! how durst you interrupt me in the most critical melting moment that ever love and beauty honoured me with?

CANTON
I demande pardonne, my Lor! Sir John Melvil, my Lor, sent me to beg you to do him the honour to speak a little to your Lorship.

LORD OGLEBY
I'm not at leisure—I'm busy—Get away, you stupid old dog, you Swiss rascal, or I'll—

CANTON
Fort bien, my Lor.—

[**CANTON** goes out tiptoe.

LORD OGLEBY

By the laws of gallantry, Madam, this interruption should be death; but as no punishment ought to disturb the triumph of the softer passions, the criminal is pardoned and dismissed—Let us return, Madam, to the highest luxury of exalted minds—a declaration of love from the lips of beauty.

FANNY

The entrance of a third person has a little relieved me, but I cannot go thro' with it—and yet I must open my heart with a discovery, or it will break with its burthen.

LORD OGLEBY

What passion in her eyes! I am alarmed to agitation.
[Aside]
—I presume, Madam, (and as you have flattered me, by making me a party concerned, I hope you'll excuse the presumption) that—

FANNY

Do you excuse my making you a party concerned, my Lord, and let me interest your heart in my behalf, as my future happiness or misery in a great measure depend—

LORD OGLEBY

Upon me, Madam?

FANNY [Sighs]

Upon you, my Lord.

LORD OGLEBY [Sighs]

There's no standing this: I have caught the infection—her tenderness dissolves me.

FANNY

And should you too severely judge of a rash action which passion prompted, and modesty has long concealed—

LORD OGLEBY [Taking her hand]

Thou amiable creature—command my heart, for it is vanquished—Speak but thy virtuous wishes, and enjoy them.

FANNY

I cannot, my Lord—indeed, I cannot—Mr. Lovewell must tell you my distresses—and when you know them—pity and protect me!—

Exit, in tears.

LORD OGLEBY [Alone]

How the devil could I bring her to this? It is too much—too much—I can't bear it—I must give way to this amiable weakness—
[Wipes his eyes]
My heart overflows with sympathy, and I feel every tenderness I have inspired—
[Stifles the tear]

How blind have I been to the desolation I have made!—How could I possibly imagine that a little partial attention and tender civilities to this young creature should have gathered to this burst of passion! Can I be a man and withstand it? No—I'll sacrifice the whole sex to her.—But here comes the father, quite apropos. I'll open the matter immediately, settle the business with him, and take the sweet girl down to Ogleby-house to-morrow morning—But what the devil! Miss Sterling too! What mischief's in the wind now?

[Enter **STERLING** and **MISS STERLING**.

STERLING
My Lord, your servant! I am attending my daughter here upon rather a disagreeable affair. Speak to his Lordship, Betsey!

LORD OGLEBY
Your eyes, Miss Sterling—for I always read the eyes of a young lady—betray some little emotion—What are your commands, Madam?

MISS STERLING
I have but too much cause for my emotion, my Lord!

LORD OGLEBY
I cannot commend my kinsman's behaviour, Madam. He has behaved like a false knight, I must confess. I have heard of his apostacy. Miss Fanny has informed me of it.

MISS STERLING
Miss Fanny's baseness has been the cause of Sir John's inconstancy.

LORD OGLEBY
Nay, now, my dear Miss Sterling, your passion transports you too far. Sir John may have entertained a passion for Msls Fanny, but believe me, my dear Miss Sterling, believe me, Miss Fanny has no passion for Sir John.
[Conceitedly]
She has a passion, indeed, a most tender passion. She has opened her whole soul to me, and I know where her affections are placed.

MISS STERLING
Not upon Mr. Lovewell, my Lord; for I have great reason to think that her seeming attachment to him, is, by his consent, made use of as a blind to cover her designs upon Sir John.

LORD OGLEBY [Smiling]
Lovewell! No, poor lad! She does not. think of him.

MISS STERLING
Have a care, my Lord, that both the families are not made the dupes of Sir John's artifice and my sister's dissimulation! You don't know her—indeed, my Lord, you don't know her—a base, insinuating, perfidious!—It is too much—She has been beforehand with me, I perceive. Such unnatural behaviour to me!—But since I see I can have no redress, I am resolved that some way or other I will have revenge.

[Exit.

STERLING
This is foolish work, my Lord!

LORD OGLEBY
I have too much sensibility to bear the tears of beauty.

STERLING
It is touching indeed, my Lord—and very moving for a father.

LORD OGLEBY
To be sure, Sir!—You must be distrest beyond measure!—Wherefore, to divert your too exquisite feelings, suppose we change the subject, and proceed to business.

STERLING
With all my heart, my Lord!

LORD OGLEBY
You see, Mr. Sterling, we can make no union in our families by the propos'd marriage.

STERLING
And very sorry I am to see it, my Lord.

LORD OGLEBY
Have you set your heart upon being allied to our house, Mr. Sterling?

STERLING
'Tis my only wish, at present, my omnium, as I may call it.

LORD OGLEBY
Your wishes shall be fulfill'd.

STERLING
Shall they, my Lord!—but how—how?

LORD OGLEBY
I'll marry in your family.

STERLING
What! my sister Heidelberg?

LORD OGLEBY
You throw me into a cold sweat, Mr. Sterling. No, not your sister—but your daughter.

STERLING
My daughter!

LORD OGLEBY
Fanny!—now the murder's out!

STERLING
What you, my Lord?—

LORD OGLEBY
Yes—I, I, Mr. Sterling!

STERLING [Smiling]
No, no, my Lord—that's too much.

LORD OGLEBY
Too much?—I don't comprehend you.

STERLING
What, you, my Lord, marry my Fanny!—Bless me, what will the folks say?

LORD OGLEBY
Why, what will they say?

STERLING
That you're a bold man, my Lord—that's all.

LORD OGLEBY
Mr. Sterling, this may be city wit for ought I know—Do you court my alliance?

STERLING
To be sure, my Lord.

LORD OGLEBY
Then I'll explain.—My nephew won't marry your eldest daughter—nor I neither—Your youngest daughter won't marry him—I will marry your youngest daughter—

STERLING
What! with a younger daughter's fortune, my Lord?

LORD OGLEBY
With any fortune, or no fortune at all, Sir. Love is the idol of my heart, and the dæmon Inrerest sinks before him. So, Sir, as I said before, I will marry your youngest daughter; your youngest daughter will marry me.—

STERLING
Who told you so, my Lord?

LORD OGLEBY
Her own sweet self, Sir.

STERLING
Indeed?

LORD OGLEBY
Yes, Sir: our affection is mutual; your advantage double and treble—your daughter will be a Countess directly—I shall be the happiest of beings—and you'll be father to an Earl instead of a Baronet.

STERLING
But what will my sister say?—and my daughter?

LORD OGLEBY
I'll manage that matter—nay, if they won't consent, I'll run away with your daughter in spite of you.

STERLING
Well said, my Lord!—your spirit's good—I wish you had my constitution!—but if you'll venture, I have no objection, if my sister has none.

LORD OGLEBY
I'll answer for your sister, Sir. Apropos! the lawyers are in the house—I'll have articles drawn, and the whole affair concluded to-morrow morning.

STERLING
Very well: and I'll dispatch Lovewell to London immediately for some fresh papers I shall want, and I shall leave you to manage matters with my sister. You must excuse me, my Lord, but I can't help laughing at the match—He! he! he! what will the folks say?

[Exit.

LORD OGLEBY
What a fellow am I going to make a father of?—He has no more feeling than the post in his warehouse—But Fanny's virtues tune me to rapture again, and I won't think of the rest of the family.

[Enter **LOVEWELL** hastily.

LOVEWELL
I beg your Lordship's pardon, my Lord; are you alone, my Lord?

LORD OGLEBY
No, my Lord, I am not alone! I am in company, the best company.

LOVEWELL
My Lord!

LORD OGLEBY
I never was in such exquisite enchanting company since my heart first conceived, or my senses tasted pleasure.

LOVEWELL [Looking about]

Where are they, my Lord?

LORD OGLEBY
In my mind, Sir.

LOVEWELL [Smiling]
What company have you there, my Lord?

LORD OGLEBY
My own ideas, Sir, which so croud upon my imagination, and kindle it to such a delirium of extasy, that wit, wine, musick, poetry, all combined, and each perfection, are but mere mortal shadows of my felicity.

LOVEWELL
I see that your Lordship is happy, and I rejoice at it.

LORD OGLEBY
You shall rejoice at it, Sir; my felicity shall not selfishly be confined, but shall spread its influence to the whole circle of my friends. I need not say, Lovewell, that you shall have your share of it.

LOVEWELL
Shall I, my Lord?—then I understand you—you have heard—Miss Fanny has inform'd you—

LORD OGLEBY
She has—I have heard, and she shall be happy—'tis determin'd.

LOVEWELL
Then I have reached the summit of my wishes—And will your Lordship pardon the folly?

LORD OGLEBY
O yes, poor creature, how could she help it?—'Twas unavoidable—Fate and necessity.

LOVEWELL
It was indeed, my Lord—Your kindness distracts me.

LORD OGLEBY
And so it did the poor girl, faith.

LOVEWELL
She trembled to disclose the secret, and declare her affections?

LORD OGLEBY
The world, I believe, will not think her affections ill placed.

LOVEWELL [Bowing]
—You are too good, my Lord.—And do you really excuse the rashness of the action?

LORD OGLEBY

From my very soul, Lovewell.

LOVEWELL
Your generosity overpowers me.—
[Bowing]
—I was afraid of her meeting with a cold reception.

LORD OGLEBY
More fool you then.
Who pleads her cause with never-failing beauty,
Here finds a full redress.
[Strikes his breast]
She's a fine girl, Lovewell.

LOVEWELL
Her beauty, my Lord, is her least merit. She has an understanding—

LORD OGLEBY
Her choice convinces me of that.

LOVEWELL [Bowing]
—That's your Lordship's goodness. Her choice was a disinterested one.

LORD OGLEBY
No—no—not altogether—it began with interest, and ended in passion.

LOVEWELL
Indeed, my Lord, if you were acquainted with her goodness of heart, and generosity of mind, as well as you are with the inferior beauties of her face and person—

LORD OGLEBY
I am so perfectly convinced of their existence, and so totally of your mind touching every amiable particular of that sweet girl, that were it not for the cold unfeeling impediments of the law, I would marry her to-morrow morning.

LOVEWELL
My Lord!

LORD OGLEBY
I would, by all that's honourable in man, and amiable in woman.

LOVEWELL
Marry her!—Who do you mean, my Lord?

LORD OGLEBY
Miss Fanny Sterling, that is—the Countess of Ogleby that shall be.

LOVEWELL

I am astonished.

LORD OGLEBY
Why, could you expect less from me?

LOVEWELL
I did not expect this, my Lord.

LORD OGLEBY
Trade and accounts have destroyed your feeling.

LOVEWELL [Sighs]
No, indeed, my Lord.

LORD OGLEBY
The moment that love and pity entered my breast, I was resolved to plunge into matrimony, and shorten the girl's tortures—I never do any thing by halves; do I, Lovewell?

LOVEWELL
No, indeed, my Lord—
[Sighs]
—What an accident!

LORD OGLEBY
What's the matter, Lovewell? thou seem'st to have lost thy faculties. Why don't you wish me joy, man?

LOVEWELL [Sighs]
O, I do, my Lord.

LORD OGLEBY
She said, that you would explain what she had not power to utter—but I wanted no interpreter for the language of love.

LOVEWELL
But has your Lordship considered the consequences of your resolution?

LORD OGLEBY
No, Sir; I am above consideration, when my desires are kindled.

LOVEWELL
But consider the consequences, my Lord, to your nephew, Sir John.

LORD OGLEBY
Sir John has considered no consequences himself, Mr. Lovewell.

LOVEWELL
Mr. Sterling, my Lord, will certainly refuse his daughter to Sir John.

LORD OGLEBY
Sir John has already refused Mr. Sterling's daughter.

LOVEWELL
But what will become of Miss Sterling, my Lord?

LORD OGLEBY
What's that to you?—You may have her, if you will.—I depend upon Mr. Sterling's city-philosophy, to be reconciled to Lord Ogleby's being his son-in-law, instead of Sir John Melvil, Baronet. Don't you think that your master may be brought to that, without having recourse to his calculations? Eh, Lovewell!

LOVEWELL
But, my Lord, that is not the question.

LORD OGLEBY
Whatever is the question, I'll tell you my answer.—I am in love with a fine girl, whom I resolve to marry.

[Enter **SIR JOHN MELVIL**.

What news with you, Sir John? You look all hurry and impatience—like a messenger after a battle.

SIR JOHN
After a battle, indeed, my Lord.—I have this day had a severe engagement, and wanting your Lordship as an auxiliary, I have at last mustered up resolution to declare, what my duty to you and to myself have demanded from me some time.

LORD OGLEBY
To the business then, and be as concise as possible; for I am upon the wing—eh, Lovewell?

[He smiles, and **LOVEWELL** bows.

SIR JOHN
I find 'tis in vain, my Lord, to struggle against the force of inclination.

LORD OGLEBY
Very true, Nephew—I am your witness, and will second the motion—shan't I, Lovewell?

[Smiles, and **LOVEWELL** bows.

SIR JOHN
Your Lordship's generosity encourages me to tell you—that I cannot marry Miss Sterling.

LORD OGLEBY
I am not at all surpriz'd at it—she's a bitter potion, that's the truth of it; but as you were to swallow it, and not I, it was your business, and not mine—any thing more?

SIR JOHN
But this, my Lord—that I may be permitted to make my addresses to the other sister.

LORD OGLEBY
O yes—by all means—have you any hopes there, Nephew?—Do you think he'll succced, Lovewell?

[Smiles, and winks at **LOVEWELL**.

LOVEWELL [Gravely]
I think not, my Lord.

LORD OGLEBY
I think so too, but let the fool try.

SIR JOHN
Will your Lordship favour me with your good offices to remove the chief obstacle to the match, the repugnance of Mrs Heidelberg?

LORD OGLEBY
Mrs. Heidelberg!—Had not you better begin with the young lady first? it will save you a great deal of trouble; won't it, Lovewell?—
[Smiles]
—but do what you please, it will be the same thing to me—won't it, Lovewell?—
[Conceitedly]
—Why don't you laugh at him?

LOVEWELL [Forces a smile]
I do, my Lord.

SIR JOHN
And your Lordship will endeavour to prevail on Mrs. Heidelberg to consent to my marriage with Miss Fanny?

LORD OGLEBY
I'll go and speak to Mrs. Heidelberg, about the adorable Fanny, as soon as possible.

SIR JOHN
Your generosity transports me.

LORD OGLEBY [Aside]
Poor fellow, what a dupe! he little thinks who's in possession of the town.

SIR JOHN
And your Lordship is not offended at this seeming inconstancy.

LORD OGLEBY
Not in the least. Miss Fanny's charms will even excuse infidelity—I look upon women as the feræ naturæ,—lawfull game—and every man who is qualified, has a natural right to pursue them; Lovewell as well as you, and I as well as either of you.—Every man shall do his best, without offence to any—what say you, kinsmen?

SIR JOHN
You have made me happy, my Lord.

LOVEWELL
And me, I assure you, my Lord.

LORD OGLEBY [Sings]
And I am superlatively so—allons donc—to horse and away, boys!—you to your affairs, and I to mine—suivons l'amour!

[Exeunt severally.

ACT V

SCENE I

Fanny's apartment

Enter **LOVEWELL** and **FANNY**—followed by **BETTY**.

FANNY
Why did you come so soon, Mr. Lovewell? the family is not yet in bed, and Betty certainly heard somebody listening near the chamber-door.

BETTY
My mistress is right, Sir! evil spirits are abroad; and I am sure you are both too good, not to expect mischief from them.

LOVEWELL
But who can be so curious, or so wicked?

BETTY
I think we have wickedness, and curiosity enough in this family, Sir, to expect the worst.

FANNY
I do expect the worst.—Prithee, Betty, return to the outward door, and listen if you hear any body in the gallery; and let us know directly.

BETTY
I warrant you, Madam—the Lord bless you both!

[Exit.

FANNY
What did my father want with you this evening?

LOVEWELL
He gave me the key of his closet, with orders to bring from London some papers relating to Lord Ogleby.

FANNY
And why did not you obey him?

LOVEWELL
Because I am certain that his Lordship has open'd his heart to him about you, and those papers are wanted merely on that account—but as we shall discover all to-morrow, there will be no occasion for them, and it would be idle in me to go.

FANNY
Hark!—hark! bless me, how I tremble!—I feel the terrors of guilt—indeed, Mr. Lovewell, this is too much for me.

LOVEWELL
And for me too, my sweet Fanny.
Your apprehensions make a coward of me.—But what can alarm you? your aunt and sister are in their chambers, and you have nothing to fear from the rest of the family.

FANNY [Weeps]
I fear every body, and every thing, and every moment—My mind is in continual agitation and dread;—indeed, Mr. Lovewell, this situation may have very unhappy consequences.

LOVEWELL
But it shan't—I would rather tell our story this moment to all the house, and run the risque of maintaining you by the hardest labour, than suffer you to remain in this dangerous perplexity.—What! shall I sacrifice all my best hopes and affections, in your dear health and safety, for the mean, and in such a case, the meanest consideration—of our fortune! Were we to be abandon'd by all our relations, we have that in our hearts and minds, will weigh against the most affluent circumstances.—I should not have propos'd the secrecy of our marriage, but for your sake; and with hopes that the most generous sacrifice you have made to love and me, might be less injurious to you, by waiting a lucky moment of reconciliation.

FANNY
Hush! hush! for heav'n sake, my dear Lovewell, don't be so warm!—your generosity gets the better of your prudence; you will be heard, and we shall be discovered.—I am satisfied, indeed I am.—Excuse this weakness, this delicacy—this what you will.—My mind's at peace—indeed it is—think no more of it, if you love me!

LOVEWELL
That one word has charm'd me, as it always does, to the most implicit obedience; it would be the worst of ingratitude in me to distress you a moment.

[Kisses her.

[Re-enter **BETTY**.

BETTY [In a low voice]
I'm sorry to disturb you.

FANNY
Ha! what's the matter?

LOVEWELL
Have you heard any body?

BETTY
Yes, yes, I have, and they have heard you too, or I am mistaken—if they had seen you too, we should have been in a fine quandary.

FANNY
Prithee don't prate now, Betty!

LOVEWELL
What did you hear?

BETTY
I was preparing myself, as usual, to take me a little nap.

LOVEWELL
A nap!

BETTY
Yes, Sir, a nap; for I watch much better so than wide awake; and when I had wrap'd this handkerchief round my head, for fear of the ear-ach, from the key-hole I thought I heard a kind of a sort of a buzzing, which I first took for a gnat, and shook my head two or three times, and went so with my hand—

FANNY
Well—well—and so—

BETTY
And so, Madam, when I heard Mr. Lovewell a little loud, I heard the buzzing louder too—and pulling off my handkerchief softly—I could hear this fort of noise—

[Makes an indistinct noise like speaking.

FANNY
Well, and what did they say?

BETTY
Oh! I cou'd not understand a word of what was said.

LOVEWELL
The outward door is lock'd?

BETTY
Yes; and I bolted it too, for fear of the worst.

FANNY
Why did you? they must have heard you, if they were near.

BETTY
And I did it on purpose, Madam, and cough'd a little too, that they might not hear Mr. Lovewell's voice—when I was silent, they were silent, and so I came to tell you.

FANNY
What shall we do?

LOVEWELL
Fear nothing; we know the worst; it will only bring on our catastrophe a little too soon—but Betty might fancy this noise—she's in the conspiracy, and can make a man of a mouse at any time.

BETTY
I can distinguish a man from a mouse, as well as my betters—I am sorry you think so ill of me, Sir.

FANNY
He compliments you, don't be a fool!—Now you have set her tongue a running, she'll mutter for an hour.
[To **LOVEWELL**]
I'll go and hearken myself.

[Exit.

BETTY [Half aside, and muttering]
I'll turn my back upon no girl, for sincerity and service.

LOVEWELL
Thou art the first in the world for both; and I will reward you soon, Betty, for one and the other.

BETTY
I'm not marcenary neither—I can live on a little, with a good carreter.

[Re-enter **FANNY**.

FANNY
All seems quiet—suppose, my dear, you go to your own room—I shall be much easier then—and to-morrow we will be prepared for the discovery.

BETTY [Half aside, and muttering]
You may discover, if you please; but, for my part, I shall still be secret.

LOVEWELL

Should I leave you now,—if they still are upon the watch, we shall lose the advantage of our delay.—Besides, we should consult upon to-morrow's business.—Let Betty go to her own room, and lock the outward door after her; we can fasten this; and when she thinks all safe, she may return and let me out as usual.

BETTY
Shall I, Madam?

FANNY
Do! let me have my way to-night, and you shall command me ever after.—I would not have you surprized here for the world.—Pray leave me! I shall be quite myself again, if you will oblige me.

LOVEWELL [Going]
I live only to oblige you, my sweet Fanny! I'll be gone this moment.

FANNY
Let us listen first at the door, that you may not be intercepted.—Betty shall go first, and if they lay hold of her—

BETTY [Going hastily]
They'll have the wrong sow by the ear, I can tell them that.

FANNY
Softly—softly—Betty! don't venture out, if you hear a noise.—Softly, I beg of you!—See, Mr. Lovewell, the effects of indiscretion!

LOVEWELL
But love, Fanny, makes amends for all.

[Exeunt all softly.

SCENE: Changes to a gallery, which leads to several bed-chambers

Enter **MISS STERLING**, leading **MRS HEIDELBERG** in a night-cap.

MISS STERLING
This way, dear Madam, and then I'll tell you all.

MRS HEIDELBERG
Nay, but Niece—consider a little—don't drag me out in this figur—let me put on my fly-cap!—if any of my Lord's fammaly, or the counsellors at law, should be stirring, I should be perdigus disconcarted.

MISS STERLING
But, my dear Madam, a moment is an age, in my situation. I am sure my sister has been plotting my disgrace and ruin in that chamber—O she's all craft and wickedness!

MRS HEIDELBERG

Well, but softly, Betsey!—you are all in emotion—your mind is too much flustrated—you can neither eat nor drink, nor take your natural rest—compose yourself, child; for if we are not as warysome as they are wicked, we shall difgrace ourselves and the whole fammaly.

MISS STERLING

We are disgrac'd already, Madam—Sir John Melvil has forsaken me; my Lord cares for nobody but himself; or, if for any body, it is my sister; my father, for the sake of a better bargain, would marry me to a 'Change-broker; so that if you, Madam, don't continue my friend—if you forsake me—if I am to lose my best hopes and consolation—in your tenderness—and affect–ions—I had better—at once—give up the matter—and let my sister enjoy—the fruits of her treachery—trample with scorn upon the rights of her elder sister, the will of the best of aunts, and the weakness of a too interested father.

[She pretends to be bursting into tears all this speech.

MRS HEIDELBERG

Don't Betsey—keep up yonr spurrit—I hate whimpering—I am your friend—depend upon me in every partickler—but be composed, and tell me what new mischief you have discover'd.

MISS STERLING

I had no desire to sleep, and would not undress myself, knowing that my Machiavel sister would not rest till she had broke my heart:—I was so uneasy that I could not stay in my room, but when I thought that all the house was quiet, I sent my maid to discover what was going forward; she immediately came back and told me that they were in high consultation; that she had heard only, for it was in the dark, my sister's maid conduct Sir John Melvil to her mistress, and then lock the door.

MRS HEIDELBERG

And how did you conduct yourself in this dalimma?

MISS STERLING

I return'd with her, and could hear a man's voice, though nothing that they said distinctly; and you may depend upon it, that Sir John is now in that room, that they have settled the matter, and will run away together before morning, if we don't prevent them.

MRS HEIDELBERG

Why the brazen slut! has she got her sister's husband (that is to be) lock'd up in her chamber! at night too?—I tremble at the thoughts!

MISS STERLING

Hush, Madam! I hear something.

MRS HEIDELBERG

You frighten me—let me put on my fly cap—I would not be seen in this figur for the world.

MISS STERLING

'Tis dark, Madam; you can't be seen.

MRS HEIDELBERG

I protest there's a candle coming, and a man too.

MISS STERLING
Nothing but servants; let us retire a moment!

[They retire.

[Enter **BRUSH** half drunk, laying hold of the **CHAMBER MAID**, who has a candle in her hand.

CHAMBER MAID
Be quiet Mr. Brush; I shall drop down with terror!

BRUSH
But my sweet, and most amiable chamber-maid, if you have no love, you may hearken to a little reason; that cannot possibly do your virtue any harm.

CHAMBER MAID
But you will do me harm, Mr. Brush, and a great deal of harm too—pray let me go—I am ruin'd if they hear you—I tremble like an asp.

BRUSH
But they shan't hear us—and if you have a mind to be ruin'd, it shall be the making of your fortune, you little slut, you!—therefore I say it again, if you have no love—hear a little reason!

CHAMBER MAID
I wonder at your impurence, Mr. Brush, to use me in this manner; this is not the way to keep me company, I assure you.—You are a town rake I see, and now you are a little in liquor, you fear nothing.

BRUSH
Nothing, by heav'ns, but your frowns, most amiable chamber-maid; I am a little electrified, that's the truth on't; I am not used to drink Port, and your master's is so heady, that a pint of it oversets a claret-drinker.

CHAMBER MAID
Don't be rude! bless me!—I shall be ruin'd—what will become of me?

BRUSH
I'll take care of you, by all that's honourable.

CHAMBER MAID
You are a base man to use me so—I'll cry out, if you don't let me go—that is Miss Sterling's chamber, that Miss Fanny's, and that Madam Heidelberg's.

[Pointing.

BRUSH
And that my Lord Ogleby's, and that my Lady what d'ye call'em: I don't mind such folks when I'm sober, much less when I am whimsical—rather above that too.

CHAMBER MAID

More shame for you, Mr. Brush!—you terrify me—you have no modesty.

BRUSH

O but I have, my sweet spider-brusher!—for instance, I reverence Miss Fanny—she's a most delicious morsel and fit for a prince—with all my horrors of matrimony, I could marry her myself—but for her sister—

MISS STERLING

There, there, Madam, all in a story!

CHAMBER MAID

Bless me, Mr. Brush!—I heard something!

BRUSH

Rats, I suppose, that are gnawing the old timbers of this execrable old dungeon—If it was mine, I would pull it down, and fill your fine canal up with the rubbish; and then I should get rid of two damn'd things at once.

CHAMBER MAID

Law! law! how you blaspheme!—we shall have the house upon our heads for it.

BRUSH

No, no, it will last our time—but as I was saying, the eldest sister—Miss Jezabel—

CHAMBER MAID

Is a fine young lady for all your evil tongue.

BRUSH

No—we have smoak'd her already; and unless she marries our old Swiss, she can have none of us—no, no, she wont do—we are a little too nice.

CHAMBER MAID

You're a monstrous rake, Mr. Brush, and don't care what you say.

BRUSH

Why, for that matter, my dear, I am a little inclined to mischief; and if you won't have pity upon me, I will break open that door and ravish Mrs. Heidelberg.

MRS HEIDELBERG [Coming forward]

There's no bearing this—you profligate monster!

CHAMBER MAID

Ha! I am undone!

BRUSH [Runs off]

Zounds! here she is, by all that's monstrous.

MISS STERLING

A fine discourse you have had with that fellow!

MRS HEIDELBERG

And a fine time of night it is to be here with that drunken monster.

MISS STERLING

What have you, to say for yourself?

CHAMBER MAID

I can say nothing.—I am so frighten'd, and so asham'd—but indeed I am vartuous—I am vartuous indeed.

MRS HEIDELBERG

Well, well—don't tremble so; but tell us what you know of this horrable plot here.

MISS STERLING

We'll forgive you, if you'll discover all.

CHAMBER MAID

Why, Madam—don't let me betray my fellow servants—I shan't sleep in my bed, if I do.

MRS HEIDELBERG

Then you shall sleep somewhere else to-morrow night.

CHAMBER MAID

O dear!—what shall I do?

MRS HEIDELBERG

Tell us this moment,—or I'll turn you out of doors directly.

CHAMBER MAID

Why our butler has been treating us below in his pantry—Mr. Brush forc'd us to make a kind of a holiday night of it.

MISS STERLING

Holiday! for what?

CHAMBER MAID

Nay I only made one.

MISS STERLING

Well, well; but upon what account?

CHAMBER MAID

Because, as how, Madam, there was a change in the family they said,—that his honour, Sir John—was to marry Miss Fanny instead of your Ladyship.

MISS STERLING
And so you made a holiday for that.—Very fine!

CHAMBER MAID
I did not make it, Ma'am.

MRS HEIDELBERG
But do you know nothing of Sir John's being to run away with Miss Fanny to-night?

CHAMBER MAID
No, indeed, Ma'am!

MISS STERLING
Nor of his being now locked up in my sister's chamber?

CHAMBER MAID
No, as I hope for marcy, Ma'am.

MRS HEIDELBERG
Well, I'll put an end to all this directly—do you run to my brother Sterling—

CHAMBER MAID
Now, Ma'am!—'Tis so very late, Ma'am—

MRS HEIDELBERG
I don't care how late it is. Tell him there are thieves in the house—that the house is o'fire—tell him to come here immediately—go, I say!

CHAMBER MAID
I will, I will, though I'm frighten'd out of my wits.

[Exit.

MRS HEIDELBERG
Do you watch here, my dear; and I'll put myself in order, to face them. We'll plot 'em, and counter-plot 'em too.

[Exit into her chamber.

MISS STERLING
I have as much pleasure in this revenge, as in being made a countess!—Ha! they are unlocking the door.—Now for it!

[Retires.

[Fanny's door is unlock'd—and **BETTY** comes out with a candle.

[**MISS STERLING** approaches her.

BETTY [Calling within]
Sir, Sir!—now's your time—all's clear.
[Seeing **MISS STERLING**]
Stay, stay—not yet—we are watch'd.

MISS STERLING
And so you are, Madam Betty!

[**MISS STERLING** lays hold of her, while **BETTY** locks the door, and puts the key in her pocket.

BETTY [Turning round]
What's the matter, Madam?

MISS STERLING
Nay, that you shall tell my father and aunt, Madam.

BETTY
I am no tell-tale, Madam, and no thief; they'll get nothing from me.

MISS STERLING
You have a great deal of courage, Betty; and considering the secrets you have to keep, you have occasion for it.

BETTY
My mistress shall never repent her good opinion of me, Ma'am.

Enter Sterling.

STERLING
What is all this? what's the matter? why am I disturbed in this manner?

MISS STERLING
This creature, and my distresses, Sir, will explain the matter.

[Re-enter **MRS HEIDELBERG**, with another head-dress.

MRS HEIDELBERG
Now I'm prepar'd for the rancounter—well, brother, have you heard of this scene of wickedness?

STERLING
Not I—but what is it?—Speak!—I was got into my little closet—all the lawyers were in bed, and I had almost lost my senses in the confusion of Lord Ogleby's mortgages, when I was alarm'd with a foolish girl, who could hardly speak; and whether it's fire, or thieves, or murder, or a rape, I am quite in the dark.

MRS HEIDELBERG

No, no, there's no rape, brother!—all parties are willing, I believe.

MISS STERLING
Who's in that chamber?

[Detaining **BETTY**, who seemed to be stealing away.

BETTY
My mistress.

MISS STERLING
And who is with your mistress?

BETTY
Why, who should there be?

MISS STERLING
Open the door then, and let us see!

BETTY
The door is open, Madam.

[**MISS STERLING** goes to the door.

I'll sooner die than peach!

[Exit hastily.

MISS STERLING
The door's lock'd; and she has got the key in her pocket.

MRS HEIDELBERG
There's impudence, brother! piping hot from your daughter Fanny's school!

STERLING
But, zounds! what is all this about? You tell me of a sum total, and you don't produce the particulars.

MRS HEIDELBERG
Sir John Melvil is lock'd up in your daughter's bed-chamber.—There is the particular!

STERLING
The devil he is?—That's bad!

MISS STERLING
And he has been there some time too.

STERLING
Ditto!

MRS HEIDELBERG

Ditto! worse and worse, I say. I'll raise the house, and expose him to my Lord, and the whole family.

STERLING

By no means! we shall expose ourselves, sister!—the best way is to insure privately—let me alone!—I'll make him marry her to-morrow morning.

MISS STERLING

Make him marry her! this is beyond all patience!—You have thrown away all your affection; and I shall do as much by my obedience: unnatural fathers, make unnatural children.—My revenge is in my own power, and I'll indulge it.—Had they made their escape, I should have been exposed to the derision of the world:—but the deriders shall be derided; and so—help! help, there! thieves! thieves!

MRS HEIDELBERG

Tit-for-tat, Betsey!—you are right, my girl.

STERLING

Zounds! you'll spoil all—you'll raise the whole family,—the devil's in the girl.

MRS HEIDELBERG

No, no; the devil's in you, brother. I am asham'd of your principles.—What! would you connive at your daughter's being lock'd up with her sister's husband?
[Cries out]
Help! thieves! thieves! I say.

STERLING

Sister, I beg you!—daughter, I command you.—If you have no regard for me, consider yourselves!—we shall lose this opportunity of ennobling our blood, and getting above twenty per cent. for our money.

MISS STERLING

What, by my disgrace and my sister's triumph! I have a spirit above such mean considerations; and to shew you that it is not a low-bred, vulgar 'Change-Alley spirit—help! help! thieves! thieves! thieves! I say.

STERLING

Ay, ay, you may save your lungs—the house is in an uproar;—women at best have no discretion; but in a passion they'll fire a house, or burn themselves in it, rather than not be revenged.

[Enter **CANTON**, in a night-gown and slippers.

CANTON

Eh, diable! vat is de raison of dis great noise, this tintamarre?

STERLING

Ask those ladies, Sir; 'tis of their making.

LORD OGLEBY [Calls within]

Brush! Brush!—Canton! where are you?—What's the matter?
[Rings a bell]
Where are you?

STERLING
'Tis my Lord calls, Mr. Canton.

CANTON
I com, mi Lor!—

[Exit **CANTON**.

[**LORD OGLEBY** still rings.

SERJEANT FLOWER [Calls within]
A light! a light here!—where are the servants? Bring a light for me, and my brothers.

STERLING
Lights here! lights for the gentlemen!

[Exit **STERLING**.

MRS HEIDELBERG
My brother feels, I see—your sister's turn will come next.

Miss **STERLING**
Ay, ay, let it go round, Madam! it is the only comfort I have left.

[Re-enter **STERLING**, with lights, before **SERJEANT FLOWER** (with one boot and slipper) and **TRAVERSE**.

STERLING
This way, Sir! this way, gentlemen!

SERJEANT FLOWER
Well, but, Mr. Sterling, no danger I hope.—Have they made a burglarious entry?—Are you prepar'd to repulse them?—I am very much alarm'd about thieves at circuit-time.—They would be particularly severe with us gentlemen of the bar.

TRAVERSE
No danger, Mr. Sterling?—No trespass, I hope?

STERLING
None, gentlemen, but of those ladies making.

MRS HEIDELBERG
You'll be asham'd to know, gentlemen, that all your labours and studies about this young lady are thrown away—Sir John Melvil is at this moment lock'd up with this lady's younger sister.

SERJEANT FLOWER

The thing is a little extraordinary, to be sure—but, why were we to be frighten'd out of our beds for this? Could not we have try'd this cause to-morrow morning?

Miss STERLING

But, Sir, by to-morrow morning, perhaps, even your assistance would not have been of any service—the birds now in that cage would have flown away.

[Enter **LORD OGLEBY** in his robe de chambre, night cap &c.—leaning on **CANTON**.

LORD OGLEBY

I had rather lose a limb than my night's rest—what's the matter with you all?

STERLING

Ay, ay, 'tis all over!—Here's my Lord too.

LORD OGLEBY

What is all this shrieking and screaming?—Where's my angelick Fanny. She's safe, I hope!

MRS HEIDELBERG

Your angelick Fanny, my Lord, is lock'd up with your angelick nephew in that chamber.

LORD OGLEBY

My nephew! then will I be excommunicated.

MRS HEIDELBERG

Your nephew, my Lord, has been plotting to run away with the younger sister; and the younger sister has been plotting to run away with your nephew: and if we had not watch'd them and call'd up the fammaly, they had been upon the scamper to Scotland by this time.

LORD OGLEBY

Look'ee, ladies!—I know that Sir John has conceiv'd a violent passion for Miss Fanny; and I know too that Miss Fanny has conceiv'd a violent passion for another person; and I am so well convinc'd of the rectitude of her affections, that I will support them with my fortune, my honour, and my life.—Eh, shant I, Mr. Sterling?
[Smiling]
What say you?—

STERLING [Sulkily]

To be sure, my Lord.—These bawling women have been the ruin of every thing.

LORD OGLEBY

But come, I'll end this business in a trice—if you, ladies, will compose yourselves, and Mr. Sterling will insure Miss Fanny from violence, I will engage to draw her from her pillow with a whisper thro' the keyhole.

MRS HEIDELBERG

The horrid creatures!—I say, my Lord, break the door open.

LORD OGLEBY
Let me beg of your delicacy not to be too precipitate!—Now to our experiment!

[Advancing towards the door.

MISS STERLING
Now, what will they do?—my heart will beat thro' my bosom.

[Enter **BETTY**, with the key.

BETTY
There's no occasion for breaking open doors, my Lord; we have done nothing that we ought to be asham'd of, and my mistress shall face her enemies.—

[Going to unlock the door.

MRS HEIDELBERG
There's impudence.

LORD OGLEBY
The mystery thickens. Lady of the bed-chamber!
[To **BETTY**]
—open the door, and intreat Sir John Melvil (for these ladies will have it that he is there,) to appear and answer to high crimes and misdemeanors.—Call Sir John Melvil into the court!

[Enter **SIR JOHN MELVIL**, on the other side.

SIR JOHN
I am here, my Lord.

MRS HEIDELBERG
Heyday!

MISS STERLING
Astonishment!

SIR JOHN
What is all this alarm and confusion? there is nothing but hurry in the house; what is the reason of it?

LORD OGLEBY
Because you have been in that chamber; have been! nay you are there at this moment, as these ladies have protested, so don't deny it—

TRAVERSE
This is the clearest Alibi I ever knew, Mr. Serjeant.

FLOWER

Luce clarius.

LORD OGLEBY
Upon my word, ladies, if you have often these frolicks, it would be really entertaining to pass a whole summer with you. But come,—
[To **BETTY**]
—open the door, and intreat your amiable mistress to come forth, and dispel all our doubts with her smiles.

BETTY [Opening the door]
[Pertly]
Madam, you are wanted in this room.

[Enter **FANNY**, in great confusion.

MISS STERLING
You see she's ready drefs'd—and what confusion she's in!

MRS HEIDELBERG
Ready to pack off, bag and baggage!—her guilt confounds her!—

FLOWERS
Silence in the court, ladies!

FANNY
I am confounded, indeed, Madam!

LORD OGLEBY [Smiling]
Don't droop, my beauteous lilly! but with your own peculiar modesty declare your state of mind.—Pour conviction into their ears, and raptures into mine.

FANNY
I am at this moment the most unhappy—most distrest—the tumult is too much for my heart—and I want the power to reveal a secret, which to conceal has been the misfortune and misery of my—my—

[Faints away.

LORD OGLEBY
She faints; help, help! for the fairest, and best of women!

BETTY [Running to her]
O my dear mistress!—help, help, there!—

SIR JOHN
Ha! let me fly to her assistance.

[**LOVEWELL** rushes out from the chamber.

LOVEWELL
My Fanny in danger! I can contain no longer.—Prudence were now a crime; all other cares are lost in this!—speak, speak, to me, my dearest Fanny! let me but hear thy voice, open your eyes, and bless me with the smallest sign of life!

[During this speech they are all in amazement.

MISS STERLING
Lovewell!—I am easy.—

MRS HEIDELBERG
I am thunderstuck!

LORD OGLEBY
I am petrify'd!

SIR JOHN
And I undone!

FANNY [Recovering]
O Lovewell!—even supported by thee, I dare not look my father nor his Lordship in the face.

STERLING
What now! did not I send you to London, Sir?

LORD OGLEBY
Eh!—What!—How's this?—by what right and title have you been half the night in that lady's bed-chamber?

LOVEWELL
By that right that makes me the happiest of men; and by a title which I would not forego, for any the best of kings could give me.

BETTY
I could cry my eyes out to hear his magnimity.

LORD OGLEBY
I am annihilated!

STERLING
I have been choaked with rage and wonder; but now I can speak.—Zounds, what have you to say to me?—Lovewell, you are a villain.—You have broke your word with me.

FANNY
Indeed, Sir, he has not—You forbad him to think of me, when it was out of his power to obey you; we have been married these four months.

STERLING

And he shan't stay in my house four hours. What baseness and treachery! As for you, you shall repent this step as long as you live, Madam.

FANNY
Indeed, Sir, it is impossible to conceive the tortures I have already endured in consequence of my disobedience. My heart has continually upbraided me for it; and though I was too weak to struggle with affection, I feel that I must be miserable for ever without your forgiveness.

STERLING [To **FANNY**]
Lovewell, you shall leave my house directly;—and you shall follow him, Madam.

LORD OGLEBY
And if they do, I will receive them into mine. Look ye, Mr. Sterling, there have been some mistakes, which we had all better forget for our own sakes; and the best way to forget them is to forgive the cause of them; which I do from my soul.—Poor girl! I swore to support her affection with my life and fortune;—'tis a debt of honour, and must be paid—you swore as much too, Mr. Sterling; but your laws in the city will excuse you, I suppose, for you never strike a ballance without errors excepted.

STERLING
I am a father, my Lord; but for the sake of all other fathers, I think I ought not to forgive her, for fear of encouraging other silly girls like herself to throw themselves away without the consent of their parents.

LOVEWELL
I hope there will be no danger of that, Sir. Young ladies with minds, like my Fanny's, would startle at the very shadow of vice; and when they know to what uneasiness only an indiscretion has exposed her, her example, instead, of encouraging, will rather serve to deter them.

MRS HEIDELBERG
Indiscretion, quoth a! a mighty pretty delicat word to express disobedience!

LORD OGLEBY
For my part, I indulge my own passions too much to tyrannize over those of other people. Poor souls, I pity them. And you must forgive them too. Come, come, melt a little of your flint, Mr. Sterling!

STERLING
Why, why—as to that, my Lord—to be sure he is a relation of yours my Lord—what say you, sister Heidelberg?

MRS HEIDELBERG
The girl's ruined, and I forgive her.

STERLING
Well—so do I then.—Nay, no thanks—
[To **LOVEWELL** and **FANNY**, who seem preparing to speak]
—there's an end of the matter.

LORD OGLEBY
But, Lovewell, what makes you dumb all this while?

LOVEWELL

Your kindness, my Lord—I can scarce believe my own senses—they are all in a tumult of fear, joy, love, expectation, and gratitude; I ever was, and am now more bound in duty to your Lordship; for you, Mr. Sterling, if every moment of my life, spent gratefully in your service, will in some measure compensate the want of fortune, you perhaps will not repent your goodness to me. And you, ladies, I flatter myself, will not for the future suspect me of artifice and intrigue—I shall be happy to oblige, and serve you.—As for you, Sir John—

SIR JOHN

No apologies to me, Lovewell, I do not deserve any. All I have to offer in excuse for what has happened, is my total ignorance of your situation. Had you dealt a little more openly with me, you would have saved me, and yourself, and that lady, (who I hope will pardon my behaviour) a great deal of uneasiness. Give me leave, however, to assure you, that light and capricious as I may have appeared, now my infatuation is over, I have sensibility enough to be ashamed of the part I have acted, and honour enough to rejoice at your happiness.

LOVEWELL [To the **AUDIENCE**]

And now, my dearest Fanny, though we are seemingly the happiest of beings, yet all our joys will be dampt, if his Lordship's generosity and Mr. Sterling's forgiveness should not be succeeded by the indulgence, approbation, and consent of these our best benefactors.

EPILOGUE

Written by Mr GARRICK

CHARACTERS of the EPILOGUE

Lord Minum	Mr. Dodd.
Colonel Trill	Mr. Vernon.
Sir Patrick Mahony	Mr. Moody.
Miss Crotchet	Mrs. —
Mrs. Quaver	Mrs. Lee.
First Lady	Mrs. Bradshaw.
Second Lady	Miss Mills.
Third Lady	Mrs. Dorman.

SCENE: An Assembly

SEVERAL PERSONS at Cards, at different Tables; among the rest **COLONEL TRILL, LORD MINUM, MRS QUAVER, SIR PATRICK MAHONEY**.

At the Quadrille Table

COLONEL TRILL

Ladies, with Leave—

2nd LADY
Pass!

3rd LADY
Pass!

MRS QUAVER
You must do more.

COLONEL TRILL
Indeed I can't.

MRS QUAVER
I play in Hearts.

COLONEL TRILL
Encore!

2nd LADY
What Luck!

COLONEL TRILL
To-night at Drury-Lane is play'd
A Comedy, and toute nouvelle—a Spade!
Is not Miss Crotchet at the Play?

MRS QUAVER
My Niece
Has made a Party, Sir, to damn the Piece.

At the Whist Table

LORD MINUM
I hate a Play-house—Trump!—It makes me sick.

1st LADY
We're two by Honours, Ma'am.

LORD MINUM
And we the odd Trick.
Pray do you know the Author, Colonel Trill?

COLONEL TRILL
I know no Poets, Heaven be prais'd!—Spadille!

1st LADY
I'll tell you who, my Lord! (whispers my Lord.)

LORD MINUM
What, he again?
"And dwell such daring Souls in little Men?"
Be whose it will, they down our Throats will cram it!

COLONEL TRILL
Oh, no.—I have a Club—the best.—We'll damn it.

MRS QUAVER
O Bravo, Colonel! Musick is my Flame.

LORD MINUM
And mine, by Jupiter!—We've won the Game.

COLONEL TRILL
What, do you love all Musick?

MRS QUAVER
No, not Handel's.
And nasty Plays—

LORD MINUM
Are fit for Goths and Vandals.
(Rise from the Table and pay.)

From the Piquette Table

SIR PATRICK MAHONEY
Well, faith and troth! that Shakespeare was no Fool!

COLONEL TRILL
I'm glad you like him, Sir!—So ends the Pol!
(Pay and rise from Table.)

SONG by the Colonel.
I hate all their Nonsense,
Their Shakespears and Johnsons,
Their Plays, and their Play-house, and Bards:
'Tis singing, not saying;
A Fig for all playing,
But playing, as we do, at Cards!

I love to see Jonas,
Am pleas'd too with Comus;
Each well the Spectator rewards.
So clever, so neat in
Their Tricks, and their Cheating!
Like them we would fain deal our Cards.

SIR PATRICK MAHONEY

King Lare is touching!—And how fine to see
Ould Hamlet's Ghost!—"To be, or not to be."—
What are your Op'ras to Othello's roar?
Oh, he's an Angel of a Blackamoor!

LORD MINUM

What, when he choaks his Wife?—

COLONEL TRILL

And calls her Whore?

SIR PATRICK MAHONEY

King Richard calls his Horse—and then Macbeth,
When e'er he murders—takes away the Breath.
My Blood runs cold at ev'ry Syllable,
To see the Dagger—that's invisible.

[**ALL** laugh.

SIR PATRICK MAHONEY

Laugh if you please, a pretty Play—

LORD MINUM

Is pretty.

SIR PATRICK MAHONEY

And when there's Wit in't—

COLONEL TRILL

To be sure 'tis witty.

SIR PATRICK MAHONEY

I love the Play-house now—so light and gay,
With all those Candles, they have ta'en away!

[**ALL** laugh.

For all your Game, what makes it so much brighter?

COLONEL TRILL
Put out the Light, and then—

LORD MINUM
'Tis so much lighter.

SIR PATRICK MAHONEY
Pray do you mane, Sirs, more than you express?

COLONEL TRILL
Just as it happens—

LORD MINUM
Either more, or less.

MRS QUAVER [to **SIR PATRICK MAHONEY**]
An't you asham'd, Sir?

SIR PATRICK MAHONEY
Me!—I seldom blush.—
For little Shakespeare, faith! I'd take a Push!

LORD MINUM
News, News!—here comes Miss Crotchet from the Play.

[Enter **MISS CROTCHET**.

MRS QUAVER
Well, Crotchet, what's the News?

MISS CROTCHET
We've lost the Day.

COLONEL TRILL
Tell us, dear Miss, all you have heard and seen.

MISS CROTCHET
I'm tir'd—a Chair—here, take my Capuchin!

LORD MINUM
And isn't it damn'd, Miss?

MISS CROTCHET
No, my Lord, not quite:
But we shall damn it.

COLONEL TRILL

When?

MISS CROTCHET
To-morrow Night.
There is a Party of us, all of Fashion,
Resolv'd to exterminate this vulgar Passion:
A Play-house, what a Place!—I must forswear it.
A little Mischief only makes one bear it.
Such Crowds of City Folks!—so rude and pressing!
And their Horse-Laughs, so hideously distressing!
When e'er we hiss'd, they frown'd and fell a swearing,
Like their own Guildhall Giants—fierce and staring!

COLONEL TRILL
What said the Folks of Fashion? were they cross?

LORD MINUM
The rest have no more Judgement than my Horse.

MISS CROTCHET
Lord Grimly swore 'twas execrable Stuff.
Says one, Why so, my Lord?—My Lord took Snuff.
In the first Aft Lord George began to doze,
And criticis'd the Author—through his Nose;
So loud indeed, that as his Lordship snor'd,
The Pit turn'd round, and all the Brutes encor'd.
Some Lords, indeed, approv'd the Author's Jokes.

LORD MINUM
We have among us, Miss, some foolish Folks.

MISS CROTCHET
Says poor Lord Simper—Well, now to my Mind
The Piece is good;—but he's both deaf and blind.

SIR PATRICK MAHONEY
Upon my Soul a very pretty Story!
And Quality appears in all its Glory!—
There was some Merit in the Piece, no Doubt;

MISS CROTCHET
O, to be sure!—if one could find it out.

COLONEL TRILL
But tell us, Miss, the Subject of the Play.

MISS CROTCHET
Why, 'twas a Marriage—yes, a Marriage—Stay!

A Lord, an Aunt, two Sisters, and a Merchant—
A Baronet—ten Lawyers—a fat Serjeant—
Are all produc'd—to talk with one another;
And about something make a mighty Pother;
They all go in, and out; and to, and fro;
And talk, and quarrel—as they come and go—
Then go to Bed, and then get up—and then—
Scream, faint, scold, kiss,—and go to Bed again.

[**ALL** laugh.

Such is the Play—Your Judgment! never sham it.

COLONEL TRILL
Oh damn it!

MRS QUAVER
Damn it!

1st LADY
Damn it!

MISS CROTCHET
Damn it!

LORD MINUM
Damn it!

SIR PATRICK MAHONEY
Well, faith, you speak your Minds, and I'll be free—
Good Night! this Company's too good for me.

[Going.

COLONEL TRILL
Your Judgment, dear Sir Patrick, makes us proud.

[**ALL** laugh.

SIR PATRICK MAHONEY
Laugh if you please, but pray don't laugh too loud.

[Exit.

RECITATIVE.

COLONEL TRILL
Now the Barbarian's gone, Miss, tune your Tongue,

And let us raise our Spirits high with Song!

RECITATIVE.

MISS CROTCHET
Colonel, de tout mon Cœur—I've one in petto,
Which you shall join, and make it a Duetto.

RECITATIVE.

LORD MINUM
Bella Signora, et Amico mio!
I too will join, and then we'll make a Trio.—

COLONEL TRILL
Come all and join the full-mouth'd Chorus,
And drive all Tragedy and Comedy before us!

[**ALL** the Company rise, and advance to the Front of the Stage.

AIR.

COLONEL TRILL
Would you ever go to see a Tragedy?

MISS CROTCHET Never, never.

COLONEL TRILL
A Comedy?

LORD MINUM
Never, never,
Live for ever!
Tweedle-dum and Tweedle-dee!

COLONEL TRILL, LORD MINUM and MISS CROTCHET
Live for ever!
Tweedle-dum and Tweedle-dee!

CHORUS
Would you ever go to see, &c.

Polly Honeycombe (1760)

The Jealous Wife (1761)
The Clandestine Marriage (1766)
The Oxonian in Town (1767)
The Manager in Distress (1780)
The Genius of Nonsense (1780)

Other works

The Plays of Terence (familiar blank verse translation)
Bonduca (adaptations of Beaumont and Fletchers play)
Epicoene (adaption of the work by Ben Jonson)
Volpone (adaption of the work by Ben Jonson)
Comus (adaption of the work by John Milton)
The Fairy Prince (wrote the libretto for Thomas Arne's masque)

He also produced an edition of the works of Beaumont and Fletcher (1778), a version of the Ars Poëtica of Horace, an excellent translation from the Mercator of Plautus for Bonnell Thornton's edition (1769–1772)

In all Colman wrote or adapted some thirty plays, and many parodies and occasional pieces.

An incomplete edition of his dramatic works was published in 1777 in four volumes.